DOUBLE
CROSSED

BRIAN WOOD

DOUBLE CROSSED

A Fighting Man Under Fire

1 3 5 7 9 10 8 6 4 2

Virgin Books, an imprint of Ebury Publishing,
20 Vauxhall Bridge Road,
London SW1V 2SA

Virgin Books is part of the Penguin Random House group of companies whose
addresses can be found at global.penguinrandomhouse.com

Penguin
Random House
UK

First published in the United Kingdom by Virgin Books in 2019
This paperback edition published in 2020

www.penguin.co.uk

A CIP catalogue record for this book is available from the
British Library

ISBN 9780753552612

Printed and bound in Great Britain by Clays Ltd, Elcograf S.p.A.

Penguin Random House is committed to a sustainable future for our
business, our readers and our planet. This book is made from Forest
Stewardship Council® certified paper.

MIX
Paper from
responsible sources
FSC® C018179

I dedicate this book to my wonderful parents who have raised me to be the person I am today.

My wife who I love so much.

My beautiful children Bailey and Charlie.

To all the men and women of our Armed Forces who have paid the ultimate sacrifice.

Lest We Forget.

CONTENTS

PROLOGUE: AN AFTERNOON AND A MORNING

14 May 2004

THE FIRST RPG that hits the Warrior shakes the armoured vehicle to a screeching halt. It's followed by a hail of gunfire, a machine-gun rat-a-tat that pings its way along the side of the vehicle. The bullets are lighter, more insistent, than the boom of the rocket-propelled grenade. Hailstones after thunder, raining down on us.

I'm in the back, in the dark. The rear of a Warrior is where the dismounts sit, poised and ready for action. It's all but black in there, the only light being one small, square window, and with the condensation, sand and grit you can see fuck all out of it. It's hot in there: a sweaty, sweltering, dehydrating heat that saps it out of you, fills the bottles you have to drink with nothing but boiling water. And with the gunfire outside, the temperature has just got that bit hotter.

'What the fuck ...?' With me in the back are Rushforth and Tatawaqa, two privates under my command as lance corporal. They're good men, loyal and true. Brave and courageous, and I know that they'll have my back, just as much as I'll have theirs. They're looking at me for an answer, but

I've got about as little clue as to what is going on as they have. I shout up to Stick, Sergeant Broome, the vehicle commander who is up in the turret, and wait for a response.

We've been in Iraq for about a month, in Maysan province. The tour was billed as a peacekeeping one, but that's turned out to be bollocks. Firefighting would have been a better description. Full-on war-fighting would have been more accurate. Over the last month, I've seen more action than in the rest of my army career put together. I've seen people pulled out of burning vehicles, colleagues being petrol-bombed, the supposed protective skin of a Warrior ripped apart by a rocket attack. I've been in hospital having almost lost my sight and been under attack from everyone from armed militia positions to ten-year-old boys.

We're fighting a militia army who doesn't want to fight it out face-to-face. When we go in to confront them with force, they slink away. They wait for your guard to come down before they bring the fight to you. They mortar us in our beds at the camp, bomb the cookhouse when we're trying to eat our dinner, send children in to do their deadly dirty work. The pace has been relentless: everyone is hot, frustrated, tired, confused. And now, here we are under attack again.

It's not even us who is meant to be under attack. We're the ones doing the rescue operation, for the troops who have been ambushed near Danny Boy, the checkpoint on Route 6 on the way to Majar al-Kabir. That town is a no-go zone for the British, ever since six members of the RMP (Royal Military Police) were cornered by an angry mob and murdered in June 2003. Today, it's like that no-go area has been extended, the town's border creeping out a few kilometres into the desert.

We haven't even made it to Danny Boy. We're God knows where out in the desert, in the middle of fucking nowhere and yet here we are, rattling around in the back of our Warrior as the RPGs and machine-gun fire rocket in. I've been fired at so many times over the last few weeks I've learned to read it pretty well. This bombardment, I know, is sustained. There's a lot of it. This isn't some loan gunman chancing his arm. The size and the volume of it tell me that the whole thing was premeditated and has been carefully planned.

Stick issues a fire control order.

Up in the turret, he and JC – Jean-Claude Fowler, the gunner – return fire. I can hear the pair of them communicating to each other as they try to work out where the attack is coming from. With a click and a 'Fuck' I can hear the chain gun jam and JC reaching for his light machine gun to continue firing.

'Woody?' Rushforth hisses. 'What's happening?'

I hold a hand up, the silhouette of which I can barely see in front of me. I want to know what is going on as much as he does, but I know that my task at this point is to be patient. You have to give the commander time, allow him to concentrate, rather than bombard him with questions. When there is finally a pause in the attack I ask Stick for an update.

'A stronghold,' he says. 'Ten, maybe fifteen militia.' Then the gun battle starts up again.

It's not nice, sitting there in the back while this continues. You have to trust that the vehicle will take it, but I've already had one episode on this tour where that wasn't the case.

'Woody.' Stick's voice crackles over the intercom. 'Prepare you and your men to dismount.'

Prepare to what? As the gunfire continues, I think I must have misheard him. Dismount? Go out in that? But Stick is serious.

'We're not having any effect here,' Stick says. 'They're in these zigzag-type trench positions. Just popping up, engaging, getting down again. Let me know when you're ready.'

'What did he say?' Rushforth and Tatawaqa look at me.

'He says we're to prepare to dismount.' As I try to reassure them, I hope they can't hear my heart smashing against my armour plate. 'We're going to get out of this vehicle and launch out on to the stronghold, okay? Standby and get ready to go.'

'There's a gully,' Stick says. 'About ten o'clock. If you go for that, I'll give you covering fire.'

We make for the door. I take the lead. 'You ready, guys?' They nod at me, but look as nervous as I feel.

'H hour,' Stick says. 'Five, four ...'

And then the door is open and I'm blinking into the bright light of the desert as my eyes readjust. The noise. Everything that has been muted and muffled in the back of the Warrior now comes into sharp, deafening focus. The kickback from the gunfire is spraying sand everywhere. Ten o'clock, I remember. Stick said ten o'clock. My heart is in my mouth and I start running, sprinting across the sand for all I am worth.

4 November 2013

The air conditioning is making me cold. The holding room is fairly plain: clean and bright and quiet. Not like the click and bustle of the cameras and photographers when I arrived at the building. Through the doors I can hear the hum of the main inquiry room. Lawyers and clerks talking and taking their designated seats at various desks, complete with rows of computers being switched on and fired up. The public gallery opposite, full of the media and other interested parties. I haven't got anyone there, didn't want to bring anyone with me. This is something I need to do on my own.

On the table in front of me is a mid-blue A4 ring binder. In it are all of the various statements I have given about what happened nine and a half years ago. The first statement I gave to the RMP in the days after the battle. That was in Camp Abu Naji. I was on rotation, part of the QRF (Quick Reaction Force), on five minutes' notice to move. The second statement I gave months later, when I was pulled out of a training course in Brecon, sat down in front of a computer screen and shown a load of photographs to identify.

The third statement I gave more recently, to the lawyers assigned to represent me at this inquiry. That statement was the most painstaking of the lot: a real back-and-forth process with every detail queried, each change initialled and signed by me. I thought that would be as far as it would go. But then came the call asking me to come to London from Paderborn in Germany, where I am currently serving with my regiment.

And so, on a cold, crisp November morning, here I am. On the train into London, I could have passed for a commuter. The only thing that marked me out from the other suits is the blue-yellow-blue of my regimental tie. I didn't take much of the journey in to be honest. Nor the Underground, nor the walk to my solicitor's office. It was all a bit of a blur.

I'm shivering a little. I don't have an overcoat with me and haven't had anything to eat. All I've had this morning is a bottle of water. I can't have breakfast when I'm nervous, and I'm as nervous as hell. Sounds a strange thing to say, but I'd be more comfortable out on the battlefield with people firing at me than what I'm about to face this morning. That's the sort of enemy I know how to handle. This one, I don't know where to begin.

There are people in that inquiry room who want to bring me down. Lawyers with small glasses and big reputations, who have levelled all sorts of accusations against me and my fellow soldiers. Mistreatment. Mutilation. Murder. They've compared our behaviour in Iraq to the Japanese in the Second World War, the Americans at My Lai. In the papers, a lawyer described the events that day as 'one of the most atrocious episodes in British Army history'.

Those lawyers are out there, lying in wait like the militia in the Iraqi desert, ready to ambush me. My lawyer is out there, too, the one assigned to represent me. We've been through my statement together, discussed what I might be challenged on. *Keep your answers short*, my lawyer told me. *Stick to the facts. They'll want you to talk, wait for you to trip up over your own words. They're going to try and goad you, make you angry, force you into saying something you don't want to say.* It's combat-fighting of a kind, but on their terms, not mine.

Elsewhere in the inquiry room is the lawyer from the MoD (Ministry of Defence). She's been in to say hello and introduce herself. That's the first time anyone from the ministry has spoken to me about this whole inquiry, five minutes before I'm due to give evidence. I'm surprised and shocked by that. I thought after everything I'd been through that I'd get a bit more support than that. But no, they've kept their distance, left me to fend for myself. I know I can't depend on her to step in and intervene if the questioning gets tough, she has other interests that she is there to represent.

There's another document in my ring binder. It's a citation. 'ASI Subject to Confidentiality' it says across the top. It says 'Restriction – Honours' underneath, then 'LANCE CORPORAL WOOD' in block capitals. The citation then summarises a series of incidents in Iraq and my part in them. 'Deserves recognition' the final paragraph reads. 'Leadership, courageous and selfless acts ... Demonstrated the highest virtues.'

That citation led to me being awarded the Military Cross. The day I went to Buckingham Palace to receive it from the Queen was one of the proudest days of my life. *You must wear this with pride*, she told me. But now, all of this – my reputation, my livelihood, my life – is on trial. I'd asked my lawyer what the consequences of today might be. Among my questions about my career, about prison, I wanted to know could I be stripped of my honours?

There's a knock on the door. An usher tells me it is time. I need to be escorted into the inquiry room, up into the dock where I'll sit for the session, ready for the arrival of the chairman. I don't know much about him, whether he'll be friendly or aggressive. The only thing I've found out about him from the Internet is that he was the judge for the trial of Dr Harold Shipman. I don't know what to make of that, but I can't believe that's a positive omen.

The door opens and I'm escorted into the inquiry room, blinking into the flicker of the computer screens as my eyes try to take everything in. The silence. I'm acutely aware of how everyone is watching me as I walk up to the dock. They always say in court cases that juries make up their minds whether someone is innocent or guilty in the first ten seconds. As I look round the room, the lawyers, the journalists, the public, I wonder what judgement they are making of me. My heart is in my mouth, each slow step feeling like I'm walking through treacle, towards the dock and the most difficult three hours of my life.

CHAPTER ONE

KICKING OFF

I DIDN'T WANT to be a soldier when I was growing up. I was desperate to be a footballer.

When I was little, I was one of those boys who couldn't stop playing. The jumpers-for-goalposts, kickabout-in-the-street kind of kid. My best mate Russell, who lived up the road, was football crazy as well. He had a big garden with a goal in it and he had an elder sister, Zoe, who was going out with this guy, Maik, who was an incredible goalkeeper. Maik, in fact, was Maik Taylor, who went on to play professionally for a string of clubs including Southampton, Fulham and Birmingham and kept goal for Northern Ireland for over a decade. Back then, he was Russell's sister's boyfriend, a soldier in the REME (Royal Electrical and Mechanical Engineers) and a great person to have a knockabout with. There were these centre lights in the garden that lit it up like floodlights, so we'd play all hours, as late as we were allowed, until I got the call to come home and go to bed.

It wasn't long before Russell and I joined a team – Headley Under 10s, which was a local village side. We were both decent players and there was another kid as well, John Edwards, who was also really good. We soon got picked up and went to play for Aldershot and from there we had trials to play for Hampshire. All three of us were selected, which is kind of amazing when you think about it, all being from the same small place. The county team meant a lot of travelling, we'd travel all over the south playing against Surrey or Devon or whoever. That was a fantastic experience and we played some amazing games. From there – I was 11 or 12 at this point – I got the chance to go for trials again, this time to try out for Chelsea.

Back then Chelsea weren't quite the club they are now. This was the early 1990s and they were just about to start the evolution on the pitch that began with Glenn Hoddle and Ruud Gullit as managers. But they were members of the newly formed Premier League and getting to play for them would be an amazing opportunity. Once again, it was me, Russell and John who all went for it, along with Ben Meakins, who was the Aldershot goalkeeper.

The trials took place in this big stadium facility on the outskirts of London – a football pitch with a running track wrapped around the outside. There were so many people there and so many different age groups that we played in 20-minute periods, had a break, played another 20 minutes, another break, another 20 minutes, done. Before the trial had started, my dad had tried to give me some advice. *Just do the basics right*, he told me. *Get the ball, don't give it away, just play football.*

That's easier said than done when you're trying to impress. But I did my best, tried to concentrate and do the simple things well. But then, about halfway through the session, the ball came over to me, a good pass. I'm a left-footed player and can hit the ball okay, so rather than listen to my dad, I just went for it. I hit this shot from about 25 yards out, caught it cleanly and it just flew. Ben Meakins was playing for the other side and it just whistled past him and smashed in against the stanchion. As soon as that went in, I was certain I had done enough. Sure enough, while Russell, John and Ben didn't get the call-up, I was offered a place to join Chelsea's School of Excellence. For a football-mad kid, you can imagine how exciting that was.

We trained during the week and played matches at the weekend. After one game against West Ham, I remember Dennis Wise, who was the club captain then, coming in to see us. He gave us this inspirational talk, told us to keep at it, train hard and that it would all be worth it in the long run. But much as I wanted that to be true, the problem was that from where we were living in Hampshire, I was struggling to make the training each week. It started at 7pm, but by the time Dad had finished work, picked me up and we'd sat in traffic on the M25 to get there, it was more like 7.30pm before I got there. Training was only an hour long, so I was missing a big chunk of it each week and getting behind. In the end, my dad went in to see the coaches to talk about it. He had an important position in the military, so it just wasn't possible for him to get away from work earlier. In the end, we all agreed that it wasn't working and that although Chelsea was an amazing opportunity, it would be better if I tried to play football nearer to home.

I had trials for Reading, then a First Division (now Championship) side, and was delighted to be accepted by them. I went straight into the team and had an incredible time. In my first year with them, I finished as top scorer, despite the fact that I played from midfield. In my second year, I was progressing well enough that they asked me to play in the year group above – so for the under 16s, even though I wasn't yet 15. At that age, being just a year older can make a big difference physically, but I knuckled down and learned to cope.

The pinnacle of the youth system at a football club was to get taken up on a YTS (Youth Training Scheme) place on leaving school, which was the last step before being offered a professional contract. Reading had two academies – North and South – and the system culminated in a match between the academies, after which those chosen to join the YTS scheme were selected.

The day of the match came and it was pissing down. That didn't help for playing good football and for all my goals and great games over the previous few seasons, I didn't have the best of matches. I didn't play badly, but I knew I hadn't shown everything I could do. My side got beaten, 3–2 I think it was, then we went inside out of the rain, had a shower and waited for the decision.

One after another, players were called in to see the coaches, who were sat waiting for us in a Portakabin. They sat me down and told me what a pleasure it had been to see me grow and excel while part of their School of Excellence. *But,* the coach continued, *I'm afraid we're not going to take you on.* The reason they gave was my build, that I was too skinny and too lightweight on the ball. *We have got someone else in your position,* the coach said, *who is a lot stronger and more developed. So we are going to go with him.*

I was devastated. Massively so. My dad couldn't believe it either. It seemed so unfair – I'd worked so hard, yet however well I'd played my physique counted against me. All players grow and develop as they get older, but I guess they couldn't see that happening anytime soon with me and decided not to take the risk. Football back then was possibly a bit more of a physical game. Stronger, more muscly players, the Mark Hughes type, were more suited to that. These days, I suspect, things are a bit different. They might have told me to go off and do some gym work to bulk out, or they might not have minded anyway as smaller, lighter players have become more important.

But back then, none of that came into play. I was let go and my dreams of being a footballer were over. I was 16 and without a clue what I wanted to do with my life. And that's how I ended up following in my family's footsteps and joining the army.

Being a soldier is in my family's blood. In fact, there has been over a hundred years of unbroken service in our family. My dad's father served out in India. My mum's father, he was with the Highland Light Infantry and was at Dunkirk during the Second World War. My father joined the Royal Highland Fusiliers, as indeed did many of his brothers. He came from a big family – nine brothers and three sisters. At one point, I think there were five or six brothers serving in the Royal Highland Fusiliers at the same time. My older brother, Gavin, he'd also gone and signed up, joined 1 SCOTS. So a career in the army seemed the logical thing for me to do.

My dad, he had a tough upbringing and that shaped who he was. He grew up in a three-bedroom council house in Springburn, a rough council estate in Glasgow. He was one of the youngest of the family. He shared a bed with five of his brothers and had to fight for his food. You had to eat your dinner fast or someone would take it off your plate. They lived on spam, so much so that he can't eat it any more, can't even look at the stuff.

Money was tight. My dad and his sister Ruby would go out to the bus terminals and collect all the big fag ends they could find and scrape together all the tobacco for my gran to smoke. My dad's youngest brother, my Uncle Douglas, would rob the TV meter for money to buy food, though most of the time the meter was already empty. One Christmas, there was no money for any presents, so one of my dad's other brothers, Uncle John, broke into Woolworths and made sure that everyone got a gift.

Dad joined the army. He worked his way up through the ranks and ended up as a WO2 (warrant officer class 2). He was mad on his fitness and instilled that in me as well. He would take me out as a young boy to do these endless hill reps, get me running and get me fit. He was a good footballer himself – a central midfielder, a box-to-box machine – and played with passion and fire.

Joining the army got him away from home, but the hardness he experienced there continued in the military. He lost his mate to an IRA ambush in Northern Ireland. He'd been out patrolling in Crossmaglen. My dad's section and his mate's were covering each other across open ground when there was gunfire. My dad was tasked to stop all traffic in and out of town. He then got a message over the radio to say that two men were down. His friend had been killed by the IRA. The military funeral that followed was something that will stay with him for ever. My dad couldn't bring himself to go back to his friend's graveside until the fortieth anniversary of his death and he laid a poppy wreath.

I was lucky, growing up, in how supportive my parents were to me. My dad, he really helped with the football, spent countless hours driving me to training and back again, stood on the touchline each game, often in pouring rain. That time spent helping me meant he didn't get as far as he could have done in his own career. My mum, too, she couldn't have been kinder and more supportive. She worked really hard as well, at one point she even had three jobs on the go to help look after us. I remember on one occasion I wanted this pair of Kickers. I was desperate to have them so she took out a catalogue loan so we could buy them. All these little things I remember and appreciate so much.

But having failed to make the grade at football, joining the army seemed the obvious step for me. That was what my brother Gavin had done and he and my dad would sit at the dinner table and discuss military stuff. Because I'd been focusing on my football, I hadn't been able to join in and always felt a little bit jealous of that connection. Now, I felt, this was my chance to sit down at the dinner table beside them.

I'd left school at 16 and had been working in a warehouse, stacking tyres. I didn't want to do that for the rest of my life, so I went off to visit the Army Careers Office in Aldershot by myself. I didn't tell my mum and dad I was going. I wanted to find out about it by myself, make my own decision on it. The guy I spoke to there, the recruiter for the PWRR (Princess of Wales's Royal Regiment), couldn't have been nicer or more helpful. We talked about my football and he told me how the army had teams, how if I was good at sport, I could end up playing for them. He told me, too, that if I joined I would see the world, could end up being sent to all sorts of locations in my work. But above all, he told me about belonging. *You'll feel part of something*, he told me. *You'll be fighting alongside some of the bravest men you'll ever meet in your life – the regiment was nicknamed the Tigers for a reason. You'll forge relationships that will be with you for life*, the recruiter said. *You'll end up leaving the regiment one day, but being part of the regiment will never leave you.*

I was sold. I wanted to sign up there and then, but because I was still sixteen (about three months short of my seventeenth birthday), I had to have a parent's signature to do so. I went back and decided to tackle my dad first. When I said I'd been at the recruitment centre, he looked at me blankly.

'What do you mean?' he asked.

'I've just been to Aldershot and I am going to join the army,' I told him. 'The Princess of Wales's Royal Regiment.'

'The Princess of what?' Dad pulled a face. 'Who the fuck are they?'

Dad hadn't heard of the PWRR, so he went to look them up. It turned out that the PWRR was a relatively new regiment, coming into being in September 1992, but the components it was made up of – the Queen's Regiment and the Royal Hampshire Regiment – had roots going back to the sixteenth century. The PWRR is an infantry regiment and has a full complement of Warrior Infantry Fighting Vehicles (1 PWRR) as well as being trained in close combat and fighting on foot (2 PWRR). Its role is 'to hold the ground and continue to take the fight forwards', bringing together soldiers from all over the south-east of England.

When my dad found about the history of the regiment, he was impressed.

'So who is going to tell your mum?' he asked.

'I thought you could,' I said.

Dad shook his head, because he knew what her reaction would be. 'No way. You can do that.'

Oh fuck, I thought. But I went through to the kitchen where my mum was cooking dinner and told her.

'You're joking me,' was her response. When it became clear that I wasn't, she said, 'You don't need to do that.' Then she added, 'Why don't you wait a while? You're only sixteen. You're really young to make that sort of decision.' I think for my mum it was difficult, not only having had a lifetime of my father in service, but now potentially both of her sons, just leaving my sister Donna. But my mind was made up and I wouldn't be shifted. Stacking tyres or seeing the world? It was a bit of a no-brainer.

At age 16 years and 9 months, my parents gave me a lift to Liphook station. I had this sausage bag slung over my shoulder with all my gear in. I said goodbye to them and got on the train to begin the journey to Bassingbourn Barracks near Peterborough where I would start my training. As the train pulled out of the station, my parents waving me off, I was nervous but excited. The next stage in my life was about to begin.

CHAPTER TWO

BOY SOLDIER

MY ARMY TRAINING began at Bassingbourn in September 1997. That was general training, the basics of being a soldier, and you did it with all the other recruits in your division. The PWRR is part of the Queen's Division, alongside the Royal Regiment of Fusiliers and the Royal Anglian Regiment. You train there for a few months and then you go on to Catterick in North Yorkshire. That second lot of training is trade specific, so focused on infantry for me. Once you've completed 24 weeks of training, then you are ready to go and join your particular regiment.

When I got to Bassingbourn, I was one of the youngest recruits. 'Boy Soldier', the others called me. Actually those in charge didn't even call me that: I had a number on my arm. You are not a name, you're a number, that was how it started, making clear who was in charge. They put you through your paces – a lot of physical training. Thankfully, all those years of doing training with Dad, those hill reps, put me in good stead. I really enjoyed that physical side and that sense of being paid to train. I liked the fact that I was being tested and pressured on that score. The fact that I was in decent shape gave me a head start. Some of the other recruits really struggled and they got it in the neck from the instructors – back-squadded, as it was called.

It wasn't just physical training that we did. There were different knowledge tests, a lot of learning about regimental core values and military history. We did weapons training, drill for discipline. All the basics on which being a soldier is built. I missed home in those first few weeks. I wasn't homesick as such, but I would call my dad every other day and tell him about the training we'd been doing. As the weeks went on, I got a real sense of that belonging the recruiter had talked about. Being with people the same age as you, going through the same emotions, you really found yourself bonding with each other. That togetherness really helped in supporting each other and pushing you to go that bit further.

After 19 weeks at Bassingbourn, in early 1998 I went on to Infantry Training Centre Catterick. Here the training was more fine-tuned and focused on your particular trade. For me, that was infantry, being a front-line soldier. That was what I had my heart set on, rather than becoming a technician, say, or a mechanic. I wanted to be the tip of the spear, so to speak. At Catterick, that's what I trained to do. They really put you through your paces there. Compared to Bassingbourn, the training all went up a gear. It was more demanding, both mentally and physically, and they pushed you hard. Whereas at Bassingbourn there was quite a bit of that 'You're not a name' stuff, shouting and screaming at you that you learned to suck up, Catterick was more about drilling discipline into you, fine-tuning your skills.

Once I'd finished my training in June, I went to join up with my regiment. At the time they were based in Canterbury as part of 5 Airborne Brigade. They were actually on rotation in Northern Ireland, somewhere that Dad had spent a number of tours in the 1970s, and my brother, too, had spent a long time there. It was marching season in Northern Ireland and so they were sent out there on rotation, making up a QRF should anything happen. But army rules dictate that you're not allowed to go on tour until you are eighteen and because I was still about seventeen and a half, I didn't go. In fact, funnily enough, I never got to serve in Northern Ireland. By the time I was old enough, that period of going there on tour had come to a close.

Canterbury was a great place to be based. It is a lovely city. As well as the obvious attractions, there were a lot of bars and pubs and a decent nightlife. Having grown up in a small village, this all seemed like fantastic fun. I was careful, mind. My dad said to me, *Remember that you're going into a rigid and structured organisation. Don't open your mouth, don't say the wrong thing. Keep your head down for the first six months and you'll be on to a winner.*

The other bit of advice my dad gave me was to make sure that I kept fit. *If you are fit, you'll be sorted*, he said. What you didn't want was to find yourself singled out as a weak link at the start. Once that happened, and you identified yourself as a potential target, that's when you would start attracting unwanted attention. I knuckled down, made sure I was always in the top ten of any physical exercises that we did and I was left alone.

In fact, the only way I didn't keep my head down was with my football. People had heard on the grapevine that I was half-decent and it wasn't long before I was being picked to play for the regiment, Infantry and then on to the army side. In terms of my fellow soldiers that really helped in getting respect right from the off. Unfortunately, it also meant that I got singled out by my sergeant major. He hated football, absolutely hated it. And he hated, too, the fact that I'd get wrapped up in cotton wool before a game, as he saw it. These notes would come down from the powers that be to take me off guard duties. While everyone would be doing their guard shift, he'd have to let me off mine.

I dreaded going to see him about it. Every time I got a letter saying that I'd been requested by the Army Football Association to play in a match, I'd have to take it to him in his office to get signed off.

'What the fuck do you want?' he'd snap at me.

'I've got a football match I need to play in Sir,' I'd say, showing him the letter.

The sergeant major, as all sergeant majors do, had a pace stick. This was used, as the name suggests, to measure out a pace. But rather than using it for that, my sergeant major would use it like a javelin and throw it at me.

'A football match? Fuck off.' And I'd duck as he launched this stick in my direction. Then I'd slide away and find my sergeant, who would give me permission to go.

On another occasion, the battalion was down to go to Lydd and Hythe ranges, for a large live-firing exercise. This clashed with an army football match, but the match was part of the build-up for some important event and so that took priority. I'd mentioned it to my platoon sergeant and he said to leave it with him. The sergeant major, well, you can guess what his reaction was and he told me to do the exercise. The buses arrived to take us to the ranges and I had my kit all packed, loaded in the luggage compartment under the bus.

The platoon sergeant came on to the bus, which was completely packed with the rest of C Company.

'Wood?' he asked. 'Wood?'

Everyone went silent as I put my hand up. 'Yes Sergeant?'

'Get off the bus, Wood, you're going to play football for the week.'

The whole bus erupted at that. As I tried to get off everyone was kicking out, trying to give me a dead leg or fill me in as I went past. I got my kit out from under the bus and as it started to pull away I just gave everyone this big double thumbs up sign. They responded with a slightly different sort of hand gesture.

That first sergeant major, he was pretty old-school. As far as he was concerned, me going off to play football was just a bit of swanning around. *You signed up to be a soldier, not to kick a ball about.* But playing for the army side was a big deal and great PR for the regiment. When he moved on and a new sergeant major took over, he got that straight away. He was much more helpful. *Let me know what you need*, he said to me, *and I'll sort it*. Rather than being seen as a hindrance by the hierarchy, my football helped me get noticed and people in the Corporals' Mess and Sergeants' Mess knew who I was. All of which made my life a lot easier in those early years of being a soldier.

Everyone on the football side knew who my dad was. *You're Wood's boy?* they'd say. They knew him as a player and also as a coach. He had a reputation for being this real fitness animal and that helped me with the coaches and getting on there. My brother, he was a decent player as well and we even played for the Infantry side together on occasion. Gavin's really talented and could have played at a higher level if he'd put his mind to it. But while I'd take it easy before a game, go to bed early to ensure I had plenty of rest, Gavin would be out on the town, rolling in at three in the morning.

Some of the football tours I went on with the army were amazing. On one occasion I was picked in the squad of 24 to go down and tour South Africa. We played in Pretoria, went to Sun City, this huge resort, were taken out on a day–night safari. We also went to Soweto and visited the shanty towns, escorted by this big police convoy. That was a real eye-opener for me, seeing the poverty and the contrast in lifestyles that could exist in the same country.

On another occasion, we got to go to Brazil, which is obviously a dream for any footballer. We trained and played near to Sugarloaf Mountain, where England would go on to have their training camp for the 2014 World Cup. Fuck me, it was hot. I remember playing a match there against the Brazilian Army and they had us running around like ragged flies. They were so talented, too. I remember being right on the halfway line, when this player came up, got the ball, stood on it and spun it up. It went up his leg, then he rolled it over on to his back, round his neck and brought it down. I looked at him as if to say, 'You are fucking joking.' Then he was sprinting off on another attack while I was trying to catch my breath.

We couldn't compete with the Brazilians individually, but what we did have was a better sense of team structure. We were more organised as a unit and that helped keep us in the games. One of the main memories I have of that tour is playing beach football against a local side. The football nets were all out there, left on the beach in perfect nick – they would get trashed in this country. But Brazilians love their beaches, love their football, so these nets stayed up in pristine condition. I think I only touched the ball once in that match, when we kicked off. The Brazilians played on the sand like we played on grass. A real masterclass. It was an amazing experience to have been part of.

Back in the UK, I played for the army development squad against a Scottish FA side. I got man of the match that day and afterwards it turned out that there had been a scout there, for Rangers. I was asked if I would go up and have a trial with them, which my regiment very kindly let me do. I don't think my original sergeant major would have been so forthcoming. Or maybe he would have been, in the hope of getting rid of me!

I went up and spent a week training with their reserves. It was a fantastic experience and a real insight into how another professional team set up and practise. Ultimately, the trial ended the same as my experiences with Chelsea and Reading: close, but no cigar. But I was comfortable with that. I'd enjoyed myself but my heart was in the army now and particularly with my regiment. I was aware that while I'd been away on these various football tours, I'd been missing out on stuff back in the UK.

The army had delivered everything that the recruiter in Aldershot had promised: I'd played my sport, I'd seen the world, I'd experienced that sense of belonging. But I'd also joined to see some action and was desperate to experience that. As the millennium drew to a close and a new one began, I was about to get my wish. And then some.

CHAPTER THREE

KOSOVO

MY FIRST TOUR was to Kosovo in 2000. I was twenty years old. Kosovo has been described as the last war of the twentieth century. It was the culmination of ongoing tensions between the ruling Serbian authorities and the majority of Muslim Albanians who lived in the province. Following the breakaway from Yugoslavia of Bosnia, Croatia and Slovenia, the KLA (Kosovo Liberation Army) was set up for Kosovo to follow suit. Serbia, though, was determined to maintain hold of the province and protect the rights of the Serbian minority that lived there.

In 1998, the Serbian police and Yugoslav Army attempted to crush the growing strength of the KLA. The result was a refugee crisis as Kosovan-Albanians attempted to flee the scene, with stories of massacres and ethnic cleansing rife. The result was that, in March 1999, following the breakdown of international peace talks, NATO opted to intervene, targeting first Serbian forces and latterly Belgrade itself in a number of airstrikes. Three months later, the then Yugoslav president, Slobodan Milosevic, agreed to withdraw his troops. A (KFOR) Kosovan Force was set up under the auspices of the UN to restore order and allow for the 1 million displaced Kosovan-Albanians to return home.

This implementation force included troops from a number of NATO countries, including the UK, and I was deployed to join it in 2000.

While the Kosovo conflict had been playing out, I had been earning my initial spurs in the army. After getting into the regiment, I spent time in Canterbury as part of 5 Airborne brigade and after just less than a year with them, was posted to Tidworth as Armoured Infantry. Here, my training continued, including learning how to drive a Warrior.

They're a decent bit of kit and rapid as well; when they get up steam and go flat out, they can really shift some. But they take a bit of getting used to because of the sheer size of them and particularly because you are only in a small driver's hatch. They're 33 tonnes and not the easiest of things to manoeuvre. The training you do is on normal roads, so there's a bit of pressure there not to crash into anything. In theory you've got road mirrors, though mine always seemed to blow in, so you were left with the commander shouting at you where to go and how you needed to readjust.

I'd only just passed all that when word came through that we were going to be deployed to Kosovo as part of the peacekeeping force. I was really excited. I joined the military and my regiment to protect and serve my country. Going on operations was the most exciting part of that. Yes, of course you wanted to go and see the world, but above all, you wanted to be operational. I was lucky, in some senses, to get to see action so early. I couldn't wait to go out there and receive my first medal.

We went into pre-deployment training. This involved basic soldiering, which included tactics, planning, first aid and counter-terrorism. The situation in Kosovo was filtered back down to us. Soldiers who'd already been out in Kosovo would come back to advise and guide us on what was happening and what the best practices were. Having that knowledge and information straight from theatre was really important. We'd get intel reports passed down to tell us about the atmospherics, the current situation on the ground, but having someone talk you through the situations you were likely to face was always invaluable.

The armoured vehicles were all sent out on boats to Greece. We then flew out to meet them and drove them in a convoy through Greece and Albania to Kosovo. That first tour, we were based in Podujevo, a town close to the border with Serbia and about 20 miles or so north of the Kosovan capital of Pristina. It was a three-pronged tour, in that we had three locations that we rotated round each fortnight: first, we were based in camp as a QRF; second, we were based in the town's police station, offering protection to some of the city's residents; on the third rotation we were based at Gate 3, which was on the border crossing between Kosovo and Serbia.

The police-station billing was perhaps the most curious of the three. With NATO having originally intervened to protect the majority Muslim population from Serbian forces, we were now there to protect the remaining Serbian minority from possible reprisals. We'd travel out into the city on reassurance patrols, creating a footprint out there on the streets and making it clear we were around. We were also given protection duties on some elderly Serbian ladies who were still living in the city. The Podujevo population had been massively Kosovan-Albanian before the war. After it, a good percentage of the Serbians who lived there had fled, but the elderly ladies we were tasked to look after were either too old or too stubborn to go anywhere else.

We called them our grannies. There was one in a flat and another in a house, which teams of four of us would take turns to look after. In the granny flat, we almost never saw the person we were protecting. For weeks, I thought we were guarding an empty flat, until one morning she briefly appeared. Wow, we thought. She is alive. Then we never saw her again.

The granny house was an odd gig. We had a Portaloo that we put up in the garden and kipped in her spare room. The place stank, proper honking. There were loads of cats everywhere and this flea-riddled dog that used to hang around and which she used to beat off with a bamboo sweeper she had. We'd laugh and joke about that and then she'd start smacking us around with the broom as well!

She'd give us this bread to eat. I say bread, it didn't look or taste anything like any loaf I've ever eaten. But our commander, a guy called Andre Pepper, said we should eat it in order to be respectful. *Eat it*, he told us. So we dutifully chewed our way through this revolting concoction. She smiled and asked how it was and we were all polite and gave her the thumbs up. Unfortunately, she took from that that we really liked her cooking. After that, she kept on making more and more of this 'bread', which we had to chew through or throw away when she wasn't looking.

Gate 3 was a big sangar – an observation post – on the Kosovan–Serbian border. We could see the Serbian sangar on the opposite side, 150 metres away. They'd watch us, we'd watch them and observe the border crossings in between. We stopped anyone travelling through the checkpoint and through our interpreter asked them where they were going, what they were doing in Serbia/Kosovo, when they were planning to return and so forth. We had a list in the sangar of personnel under surveillance, whose movements we needed to keep a particular eye on.

We'd check vehicles coming through to see if anyone was smuggling anything, weaponry in particular. And it wasn't just vehicles either. The odd coffin would come through with children in, which was disturbing in itself. But we had to open them up and make sure no one had trying to slip a gun in there.

We'd get build-ups of people. On occasions we had crowds gathering in their hundreds demanding to be let over the border. That was always a tense moment and we'd be talking to them via an interpreter, attempting to calm the situation down. I was ready if we were needed. As part of our pre-deployment training, we'd done lessons where we did public-order exercises. You'd have your helmets on, visors down, shields up, and get smashed with these rubber bullets and petrol bombs thrown at you. Another regiment would come in and play the local population, attempting to charge at you and break your lines. I always enjoyed those exercises, getting that sense of how you worked as a team, how to manage that controlled aggression while rubber bullets are pinging around. What you really want to do in that situation is to break the base line and charge at someone with your baton, responding in kind to the person who has just thrown something at you. But you learned how to contain that – the importance of keeping your shape and not breaking your base line.

All of these tasks we carried out as part of the British contribution, but it was a United Nations force and there were facilities for all the troops where we'd meet units from other countries. There was a place called KFOR Hill, which was a big complex full of what we called the PX, which were basically wooden stalls selling all kinds of goods. There was an American PX, French, Dutch, Danish, everything. When we got time off, we'd get a vehicle and head down there. It was always the American store you went to, they just had the best stuff, the cheapest and widest range. Everything from Gatorade to Coke in big quantities. We'd stock up on those to take them back to camp with us.

Not for the last time, I discovered that the Americans had it better than the rest of us. The temperatures on that first tour varied wildly. When we got there in the summer it had been really boiling, but as the months ticked over into winter, it started getting really cold and heavy with snow. One day, a call came in for a couple of platoons to go down into Podujevo valley, where the Americans were. There was intelligence that there was a lot of traffic in weaponry going down, so we needed to set up a number of vehicle checkpoints and search any vehicles which seemed suspicious.

We went down there in our Warriors, but once we got there we were assigned to do foot patrols. That was what we were best at and how you get the best intelligence, talking to people on the ground and getting a sense of the situation in a way that you can't do from the back of a vehicle. We were freezing and had all our arctic gear on – all the big mitts and extreme-weather hats. So there we were, wading through this deep snow up to our shins and all the time the Americans were in their Humvees, baking away with their heaters on full blast and giving us the thumbs up. I remember thinking, What the fuck is going on here? It was a bit of an eye-opener into the politics of the military and where the power really lies.

I grew up a lot on that first tour of Kosovo. At the back end of it, they ran a junior NCO (non-commissioned officer) cadre for private soldiers to be promoted to lance corporal. I got selected to go on that and it was a real thrashing for four weeks. A lot of it was geared towards fitness and most of the instructors were P Company trained and they really put everyone through their paces. It was cold, the terrain was hilly and it was hard to get through – even for someone like me, who'd always prided myself on my physical ability.

You had to be fit to be a private soldier, but to move up you had to be even fitter and more robust. We'd do a whole day-and-night-nav exercise on the hills and then would come back and be straight into the gym for a 50-minute training session. Then you had a few hours' sleep and then back out going through model drills. It was relentless in that way.

There was a leadership element to training as well. Not as much as there is now, but some real learning on what it is like to be leader – what you need to deliver on, how you command. I did all that and passed. I got promoted in a ceremony on the HLS (helicopter landing site). The CO (commanding officer) and the RSM (regimental sergeant major) came down with the OCs (officer commanding) from the companies. Becoming a lance corporal is one of the hardest promotions to earn; it is also one of the easiest ones to lose. So they make an effort over it. For me, it was the perfect end to my first tour, getting out there, being operational and coming back having been promoted. In many senses, it doesn't get much better than that.

I went back out to Kosovo again for my second tour in June 2002. This time I was based in Pristina and because of my promotion, I had more responsibilities to deal with. I had four guys to look after now. I'd get clear direction from my section commander and would then feed this back down the line to the lads, who would carry out what needed to happen.

There was more general patrolling on this tour – that was out on foot and in the Land Rovers and Warriors – and a lot more stop-and-searches of vehicles. The regiment had some good finds – big lorries full of weapons systems. A lot of the regiment had previously been out in Northern Ireland, where they'd been used to this sort of set-up and activity, but I was new to it all, so continued to learn. I spent time listening to others who had operational experience as to the sort of things to look out for.

The other main difference I remember between the two tours was that during the second, the UN held a football tournament between all the different countries that were out there. A guy called James Cameron was the CO of my regiment at the time. He was a big football fan, supported Gillingham and made sure I got involved.

There were teams from Belgium, the Netherlands, Denmark, all over. The Kosovans had a side and a number of the different British regiments had their own teams as well. There was a league system set up with groups and then the winners of each went on to progress to the knockout stages. The matches were seven-a-side, I think about 20 minutes each way. Our side was managed by Captain McCloud, a mad northerner from Manchester. He was a good old-fashioned manager, all busted nose and 'Get stuck in!' shouted from the sidelines. We had some of the REME lads in our team, so we had a good squad. We even had the official regimental kit – blue with yellow stripes – brought out to wear. I had my boots with me – I always took them out on tour – and played in my preferred position on the left side of midfield.

The tournament took place in the Kosovan national stadium, which probably makes it sound better than it actually was. It was this huge, open, concrete bowl that was falling apart. There was no roof so when it rained everyone got soaked, but it had a lot of character to it. The Kosovans were all invited to watch, so the stadium was packed with this great crowd. We had a load of footballs and old kits and stuff that we handed out to the kids who were watching. The stadium itself was ringed with soldiers and vehicles to make sure it was secure. It was all a bit surreal.

The tournament was described as a friendly one but obviously once you're in it, you really want to win. In the quarter-finals we came up against the Royal Marines and there was a real bit of rivalry there as we were both British and wanted to put one over the other. What was odd for me was that my mate Leyton Johns was playing for their side. We'd grown up in the same village together and although I knew he was out in Kosovo, this was the first time I'd seen him while out there. Afterwards, we took a photo of us together on my Warrior and sent it home for everyone to see.

We beat the Royal Marines, which was good crack, before getting knocked out by the Danes in the semi-finals. They went on to play the Kosovans in the final, which I don't think was a fix, but they had the crowd behind them and went on to win the tournament which was a great piece of PR all round. Then the next morning it was back out on the patrols.

In between the two tours of Kosovo, the whole political landscape shifted. In September 2001, I was back in the UK, training with the army football team in Aldershot. I was in the showers, when someone came in and said, 'An aeroplane has just hit the Twin Towers.'

At this point, I must confess that I didn't even know where the Twin Towers were.

'In New York, you idiot.'

I got showered and dressed and went out to watch the events unfold on TV. Because it was the army team, it was a real cross-section of soldiers from all sort of regiments there, from the Infantry to the Royal Engineers. Like the rest of the world, it was difficult to take in exactly what we were seeing.

But unlike the rest of the world, everyone in that room had a slightly different emotion. As well as the shock and horror at what we were seeing on the screen, there was a definite sense that there was going to be a response to what was happening. As the US's strongest ally, the British were likely to be there alongside her. That meant war. And that meant us.

It was a weird, mixed feeling to have. You join the military to serve and protect and you want to go on operational tours, to test yourself in extreme situations. Once you have been through that, you don't wish it upon anyone because it is so hard and demanding. But as a soldier yourself, you want to be in those situations and have the opportunity to fight for something you care about.

So on that second tour of Kosovo we followed what was happening in Afghanistan and that kind of took the edge off things. Here we were, doing foot patrols, searching vehicles and protecting grannies and there they were, taking the fight to the Taliban. We knew as a regiment we'd be unlikely to be involved in that – the IEDs (improvised explosive device) and irrigation ditches meant the terrain wasn't right for our armoured vehicles – and besides, we were already committed to being in the Balkans. So we followed events in Afghanistan and I felt extremely frustrated that I wasn't out there, in the thick of it. I wished I could have my chance to test myself in such circumstances.

As they say, be careful what you wish for.

CHAPTER FOUR

A TOUR LIKE NO OTHER

ON 5 NOVEMBER 2003, my regiment was called to a scale A parade at the large gymnasium in Tidworth. Rumours were everywhere. If there's one thing a military organisation likes, it is a rumour. If you believed everything you heard, we'd be about to be off fighting seven wars simultaneously. But obviously, expectations were high. We were in the middle of one of the most active periods that the army had seen for years, if not decades: Kosovo, Afghanistan and now Iraq, following on quickly from each other. As I said earlier, the Afghanistan terrain wasn't an obvious fit for us, but Iraq seemed like it might be. Like many of my fellow soldiers, I was hoping that we were about to get the call.

The gymnasium was packed and crackling with anticipation; the officers sat in rows at the front, the rest of us were stood up in company lines behind. After what seemed like an age, our new CO, Lieutenant Colonel Matt Maer, finally appeared. He walked to the front and up on to the stage. There were not microphones or anything, but we could all hear what he said.

'My name is Lieutenant Colonel Matt Maer,' he began, introducing himself to those he hadn't met before. 'I am your new commanding officer and in twenty weeks' time we deploy on operations in southern Iraq – it will be a tour like no other.'

It was a speech that everyone who was in that room would never forget. Maer spoke powerfully, in a way that really captured the drama of the moment. It was an inspiring talk, but also one that made clear the realities of the situation we were going to face. 'Look to your left and to your right,' he said. 'Unfortunately there are going to be people in this room who won't be returning home.' He confirmed a lot of the rumours that had been doing the rounds and gave us an overview of the situation out there at this point. Overall, the speech was stirring. *This is why we joined the military*, he told us. By the time he finished, you could hear a pin drop in that place. There were no questions, just the regimental sergeant major, Chalky White, telling us to fall out.

I was excited. Kosovo had been a great beginning, but this was the first time I was going into a situation where the environment was kinetic. It was going to test every single person in that room at some point. This was why I signed up – to go and fight for my country and be at the sharp end of things. I wasn't nervous, not at that point. I think that only really kicks in when you're getting on the plane and actually flying in.

We were going to go in at a time when the mood on the ground was changing. The Iraq War itself had been a quicker, briefer conflict than I think anyone had anticipated. Operation Iraqi Freedom, as the Americans called it, Operation Telic to the British, began on 20 March 2003. By 9 April, coalition troops had entered Baghdad and Saddam Hussein's reign had come to an end. On 1 May, the US president, George W. Bush, visited troops on board the American aircraft carrier USS *Abraham Lincoln* and declared 'Mission accomplished'.

The truth, however, was a lot more complicated than that straightforward narrative suggested. While the war was easy, the peace was to prove much more difficult. Saddam Hussein had fled the capital but remained at large in the country; it was not until December 2003 that he was found and captured. As for the weapons of mass destruction, the reason behind going to war in the first place, these were never found or discovered. And while the Iraqi people were initially jubilant at the overthrow of Saddam and his regime, the lack of American post-war planning and the vacuum on the ground that followed had started to turn the atmosphere sour. Into this vacuum, an insurgent movement started to grow. Some of these were local fighters, and some were bolstered by an Al Qaeda affiliated group, led by Abu Musab al-Zarqawi. There was a growing Mahdi Army, a Shia militia created by the cleric Muqtada al-Sadr.

Each of these groupings wanted the coalition forces out and were not only attacking them but also the newly established Iraqi Security Forces, which had been set up to restore order in the post-Saddam country. All of this was starting to come to a head in spring 2004. On 31 March, shortly before I was due to leave for Iraq, a convoy of American military contractors was ambushed by insurgents in the city of Fallujah. Four Americans were killed before their bodies were dragged out of their vehicles, then beaten, burned and hung from a bridge over the Euphrates. It was less than a year after Iraqis had cheered the coalition troops entering Baghdad, now the mood and atmosphere could not have been more different.

I remember that the 1st Battalion Light Infantry had been out in Iraq before us and for most of the time had experienced a relatively quiet tour. But towards the end, that had all started to turn, with tensions beginning to build and grow. All of that was trickling down to us, this deteriorating mood, as we continued our preparations to go. But at that point, Iraq seemed half a world away, literally so, as we went out to Canada to do our pre-tour training.

We went to Medicine Hat, to the prairie, and that's where we did our armoured training. It's pretty hideous out there, in terms of the facilities and the weather – four seasons in one day is common. But it's a good practice ground for using armoured vehicles alongside tanks. The QRH (Queen's Royal Hussars) were out there as well and we integrated with them, working on combining our firepower with their firepower, their tactics with ours. It was an eight-week stint out there on the prairies and there's not a huge amount to do. If you were lucky you got to do some adventure training. There was a notorious bar in Medicine Hat called Sin Bin that a lot of people went to. That often ended in up carnage – people getting pissed and locals picking fights, so I'd try and avoid it. When I got time off, I went down to Edmonton instead.

Back in the UK, we did more training with the Warriors on Salisbury Plain and went to Castlemartin in Wales where we conducted live firing. We did TESTEX, which is where you got tested by people from external regiments, checking the brigade and battle group on everything from planning to execution. That's to make sure that you're fit for purpose and ready to be deployed. Some people made the comment that we were going out to be deployed in the desert and here we were training in the pissing rain in Wales. But that was how it was. One of the great skills of the British Army is its flexibility (principle of war), being able to adapt to different circumstances. Acclimatisation is part of the job.

We also had a lot of specific training tailored to going to Iraq. We studied everything from section attacks to patrol lanes, first aid to IED recognitions, counter-insurgency training and dealing with prisoners of war. We also had lessons in cultural awareness. A lot of the time you'd have an interpreter with you when you were out, but it was important to know a bit of the language and we'd learn some Arabic, basic phrases that we could use when we were out and about.

As the training went on, there was the sense of it evolving the nearer we got to leaving. Originally, the tour had been earmarked as more of a peacekeeping one. That was what we'd been briefed to expect and what we'd been prepped for. But as details came back from soldiers like the Light Infantry of what the atmospherics were like on the ground, it was clear that the tour was going to be somewhat different – less peacekeeping and more war fighting. That made it a bit more real. The fact that I would be going out to that, while leaving a wife and newborn son behind, just heightened the stakes still further.

The first time I met Lucy in 2000, it was through my mate Leyton Johns. Leyton, the Royal Marine who I played against in the football tournament in Kosovo, lived just across the road from me. One day, he told me he was going to get a tattoo done.

'I've always fancied getting one done myself,' I told him.

'Well, why don't you come down to Portsmouth and get one done with us?' he suggested. 'There's a whole group of us going. It'll be a laugh.'

The day came and Leyton pulls up in his car. Apart from him there was Russell, my best mate, Lucy and her friend Jo. I didn't know Lucy at the time but I did know her sister

Amy. I remember liking Lucy as soon as I saw her and thinking she was really attractive.

It turned out it was Lucy's first time getting a tattoo as well, so we ended up getting them done together: I was getting a Scotland flag on my leg, Lucy a tribal thing at the base of her back. I think I went in first, if I remember rightly, then Lucy followed. Because my tattoo was being done on my leg, I had to take my shoes off. I had this new pair of trainers on, which Russell and Leyton got hold of and did this thing with my laces. They took them out and then did them up all cranky, which wound me up something rotten, as I tried to put them back on again. After the tattoos were done, we went down the beach at Southsea and Lucy and I got talking to each other. We hit it off well and slowly started to get to know each other.

For a bit of extra money, Lucy used to work at The Outback, which was the pub at the top of our village. I was in Tidworth at the time, so would come home at weekends and when I was on leave. I'd drive back early, while everyone else was still at work and would head to the pub to have a look in the car park. If Lucy's car was there, I would pull in and go to the bar to have a drink. She played it cool and never gave anything away about how she felt about me, so I was really grafting! One time, I asked her how many days she had at the pub that week.

'I'm working down at Wrecclesham tomorrow,' she said, 'it'll be really quiet down there.'

I was on leave at the time, so I said, off the cuff, 'I'll come down and keep you company if you like.'

She looked at me and said, 'Oh, you won't come down.'

'I will,' I said. And I did. At that point, if she had any doubts about what I thought about her, she now knew. The pub was dead and there was only me in there. I spent pretty much the whole day in there, getting to know her and at the end of it said, 'Look, do you want to go out and get something to eat?' And that was our first date.

I knew that nothing was going to happen there and then as we both had holidays booked: she went out to Turkey with her friends and I went on a boys' holiday to Magaluf. So we went off and did that and then when I got back I was on exercises with my company. I was driving my Warrior out on a night move across the Plain, all blacked out, lights off. It was really dusty, difficult to see. Anyway, one of the vehicles stopped at a junction and before I knew it we'd all smashed into the back of each other – an armoured vehicle pile-up. One of the vehicles stopped dead, another vehicle smashed into the back of that. I smashed into the back of that one and someone else smashed into the back of me.

Such was the force, I was shoved forwards and smashed my head on the steel of the hatch, splitting it open. I remember there was a ringing noise and that was it. The exercise was over, the lights were on and we tried to make sense of what had happened. I was taken to Salisbury hospital. My forehead was claret from all the blood. They had to glue my head back together and then stitch it up. I ended up having 21 stitches. They couldn't use dissolvable ones because it was so deep, so I had to go back and have them all snipped out. That scar, the line you can see across my forehead, that's what that is.

I'd been looking forward to seeing Lucy again, having not seen her because of the holidays, but when I eventually made it back to the pub to see her, I looked like this sort of Frankenstein thing – all puffed up, two black eyes and this row of stitches across my forehead.

'Oh my God,' Lucy said. 'What happened to you?'

Fortunately, my accident didn't put her off. About a month or so after that, I went out to Kosovo for the first time. Because her dad was in the military she knew a bit about what that was like and having someone go away on tour. I would write to her, 'blueys' as we used to call them then. This was the days before e-blueys, emails, so it was all letter writing. I wasn't a great letter writer and my grammar was poor. I didn't have the neatest handwriting so sometimes I'd use a ruler to help keep my writing straight, on other occasions I couldn't be bothered and my writing would be all over the place. But despite my handwriting, there was enough in what I was writing to keep her writing back. It was strange to think that I'd known Lucy longer through writing letters at that point than I'd known her in person. I suggested that when I came back for some R & R that we should go on holiday together, to Fuerteventura.

I wasn't sure what she was going to say to that. I wondered if it was a bit too soon or if it was a bit forward as I hadn't even been in the country. Plus she was three years older than me and I was really punching above my weight. But I thought I'd ask – knowing that what she said would either make or break us. To my delight, she said yes and after that we were together.

In fact, we got married pretty quickly in March 2002, before I went out to Kosovo for the second time. We had been talking about it on and off and in the end I asked her in the car. We were out driving and I turned round to her and said, 'Shall we get married then?' Then we went to the pub in our local village and had a drink. Not very romantic, I know! Now I'm older and a bit more thoughtful I probably would do things differently, but back then, I was never like that. I was only 21. I used to say to her, 'You've taken all my years away from me.' And she just rolled her eyes and was like, 'Whatever.'

I didn't go on one knee or anything, then. Mind you, that would have been difficult to do when I was driving. But I did ask her dad's permission beforehand. I remember asking Lucy's mum, Sue, 'Is Alan going to be around today? Will he be on his own?'

She was sharp as a tack and knew what that was about. 'So what's going on here then?' she asked, with this look on her face.

When I did get to speak to Alan, I told him what I was planning on doing. He shook my hand and said, 'Just make sure you look after her.' And I promised I would.

We got married in Gretna Green, over the anvil as tradition there has it. We'd been there for a wedding for one of Lucy's cousins and thought it was lovely. It's a beautiful place and because a lot of my family are from Scotland it meant that there was less travelling for them to do. Everyone else made a long weekend of it staying in cottages in and around the area. The only down note, really, was that the wedding coincided with the start of my second tour of Kosovo. I got dispensation to join the tour later, after my honeymoon, but it meant I only had three of my military mates there.

In fact, it was quite a civilian wedding. I didn't get married in uniform but wore a kilt instead. My brother was my best man. The night before the wedding it all got a bit wild. We had a bit of a blowout and everyone got steaming. I ended up in my brother's cottage, which was 10 miles away from the venue. I remember waking up and thinking, Oh, what is going on? Where have I left my sporran and my speech? But it all turned out fine and was just the most brilliant day. We had our honeymoon in the Maldives and then I was straight out to Kosovo to join up for my second tour.

By the time it was announced we were going to Iraq, Lucy and I were living together in married quarters in Tidworth and she was expecting. We'd talked about having kids and wanted them quite quickly. I wanted to be a young dad. I thought that was important, because I wanted to be able to compete with them when they were older, not to be some old dad in his chair when they wanted to go out and play football.

Bailey was a leap-year baby, born on 29 February 2004. So technically, he has one birthday every four years! Practically, we let him decide when he wants it. In a neat sort of symmetry, he was born just before my first tour of Iraq and our second son, Charlie, was born just after my second tour of Iraq in May 2009. That second birth was something of a story. We were out living in Germany at the time and Lucy's mum and dad, Sue and Alan, flew out to help us with the birth and look after Bailey. I remember that I had a Sergeants' Mess do and I had just got changed into my mess dress when Bailey came running to the door and said, 'Nan's fallen over and hurt herself.'

I ran out and there she was, sat out on this hill, ever so calm. She said, 'I've done some damage to my ankle.' I thought it was probably just a bad sprain and said, 'It'll be okay. Just don't move it.' But when we got to the hospital we found out it was broken in about a dozen places. Snapped, blown up. That all happened the day before Lucy was due to be induced. So they ended up both being in the same hospital but in different wards! Sue had an operation – plates, screws, you name it were put into her ankle and she ended up having to wheel herself across in a wheelchair to see Lucy.

We were in a normal German hospital for the induction and birth. None of the nurses spoke English and we didn't speak German, so that didn't help matters. Neither did the fact that you weren't allowed any painkillers or an epidural. Not even gas and air. We had this strict German midwife and you didn't mess with her. 'Push' she kept on saying to Lucy, which was about all we could understand. I remember standing there, feeling a bit of a spare part as all this was going on and everyone was running about. Lucy's mum would have been good in that situation. At one point, Lucy was screaming and I thought, What the fuck do I do?

Sue had been there for Bailey's birth, which really helped. It's probably easy for me to say, but that birth was relatively smooth by comparison to Charlie's. I remember Lucy having an epidural, which made a big difference. Lucy's legs got really itchy during the birth, she said afterwards that she would even have got some barbed wire and scratched them with it they were that bad. But Sue was a legend, sat there and patiently scratched her daughter's legs for her.

We'd decided not to know in advance if the baby was going to be a girl or a boy. So that was a moment and a really nice surprise when we discovered that we'd had a boy. I was overjoyed. We've been lucky to have two boys and I wouldn't change that for the world. I'd love to have a girl and have said in the past if we were guaranteed to have a girl we'd have another baby, but I wouldn't want to risk having three boys. But we've moved on from all that now. We are all settled and I wouldn't want to go back to nappies and everything at this point.

I was immensely proud at Bailey's birth, that new-dad mix of being excited and scared at the same time. It was my first time and I didn't really know what to do. I hadn't been to any antenatal classes or anything like that, so it was a real leap into the dark. I'd done that male thing of getting prepped with kit, so buying cots and buggies and things. Bailey was the first grandchild on both sides of the family, so that was a big deal. My parents, who were in Scotland at this point, came down from Edinburgh. That was a nice moment.

Lucy had some complications a few days after the birth. I was out in Guildford with a few friends to wet the baby's head, when my phone started going crazy. I'd had a few by this point but sobered up sharp when I started talking to Sue. Lucy had been taken to hospital in an ambulance, she told me. It transpired that after the birth, they left a bit of the placenta inside her. She'd started bleeding and haemorrhaging and they'd whisked her to A & E.

It wasn't a great moment. Sue was pissed with me and I was, well, just pissed. The evening had been something of a celebration, so I'd been doing shots and letting my hair down. The one stroke of luck was that I'd gone out drinking in Guildford, which was where Lucy had been taken. I remember running through the streets to the hospital, trying to sober up in the cold air, hoping that she was going to be all right. I must have looked a state when I got there.

'My wife is here,' I said, gasping between breaths. But they couldn't find her at first. They didn't have any record of her and it seemed to take an age to track her down. Eventually, they found her and took me down to the ward where she was. That was awful. I got in there and I almost didn't recognise her. By this point, she had lost so much blood she was gaunt and yellow, nothing like the Lucy I knew. She ended up in hospital for days, having blood transfusion after blood transfusion. It was scary then and it's scary thinking about it now, how much blood she lost and how close she was to bleeding out.

Just make sure you look after her. That's what Alan had said to me when I'd asked for his daughter's hand in marriage. But how could I look after her and be a father to Bailey when I was about to go out and serve in Iraq? If you were planning the timing, you probably wouldn't have had a baby a few weeks before you went off on tour, but that's life I guess. It's what happens when you're making other plans.

But it certainly piled on the pressure. I was nervous and excited about going to Iraq and what we might face there. And nervous and excited, too, at home, as to how best to be a father. I was aware of that bonding time that Lucy was going to get with Bailey that I was going to lose out on. He was so little – only a few weeks old – when I left. How could he possibly know who I was? By the time I came back, I'd be starting from scratch again.

It was a crazy time. Those first few weeks after a birth, your body clock is all over the place. Sleep patterns were out of the window as you adjusted to having a baby in the house. With that and the countdown to Iraq my head was all over the place. I was leaving Lucy to cope with Bailey by herself, which I knew was how it was, we both did, but that didn't make it any easier for either of us. And I was leaving Bailey, too, which was just so hard.

When I left for Iraq, Bailey was in his Moses basket. When I returned, he was in a cot. That always seemed to symbolise something – a whole stage of his growth I missed out on. Those precious first few months of his life that I'd never get back or get to experience for myself.

Saying goodbye to Lucy when I went to Iraq was harder than before. Partly because I was less certain what it was that I was about to go and face, but also because I was leaving both her and Bailey behind. I didn't tell her about the information that was coming down to us about what we were about to fly into. I couldn't protect her from everything, she could watch the news and see what was going on, but I wanted to shelter her as much as I could, didn't want her to worry. But I had some dark thoughts in the back of my mind for sure. What if I never came back? I would never get to know my son and my son would never have a father. That's pretty bleak and you couldn't dwell on it. You have to deal with that emotional side of the job or you'd never get out of bed. I'd tried to shut those thoughts off, but I'd be lying if I said they weren't there.

Lucy didn't come to see me off. We left at night and with Bailey being so young he needed his sleep rather than being dragged out of bed at some ungodly hour. So I said goodbye to both of them, gave them a farewell kiss, then slung my bags over my shoulder and walked out of the door, closing it behind me and heading across Tidworth to where we were meeting up.

It wasn't just Lucy and Bailey I was leaving behind. On my previous tours, I'd always taken my football boots with me. Had them there, just in case the opportunity came up. This time, however, they stayed in their bag at home. In its own small way this was indicative of the seriousness of the situation that I was about to head into.

CHAPTER FIVE

WELCOME TO IRAQ

THE JOURNEY TO IRAQ started late. From Tidworth we went to RAF Brize Norton, where we were going to get flown out from. But when we got there, everything was delayed and we ended up waiting 12 hours for the flight to take off. That was the RAF all over for you, they are never on time for anything. So the fact that we were delayed wasn't a huge surprise, but it still felt like an inauspicious start.

Eventually we flew from there to Qatar and then on from there to Basra International Airport. Qatar is just a base in the middle of nowhere, but Basra is a proper airport and it felt a bit weird landing there. As soon as we arrived, everyone was told to put on their helmet and body armour, then we were escorted on to a coach which was all blacked out with the curtains pulled shut. There was no air con and it was absolutely boiling.

Welcome to Iraq.

We were transferred to Shaibah, which was a huge base. It's where all the logistics were. REMFs as we called them – Rear Echelon Motherfuckers. Very important people, and critical to our mission, in terms of the supply chain, but the sort who didn't get as far as the front line, but instead stayed back, never venturing on beyond the wire.

For three days we were put through our paces, getting acclimatised to the heat. We'd be out running in the heat, fully kitted up to get used to that. All our weapons were zeroed, making sure that they were firing properly and hadn't been damaged in transit. We had more last-minute training – first aid and trauma lessons. We had intelligence briefings, getting right up to speed with everything that was happening on the ground.

The heat was the thing. Man, it was fucking hot – this horrible, dry, blistering heat. It got scorching during the day and cold at night. If you weren't on it, it was really easy to get seriously dehydrated. That was particularly true in the back of the Warriors. We got out there in early April, so the temperatures were touching 30–40°C. But in the back of the armoured vehicles there was no air con and it was 50°C plus in there. As soon as you stepped in one of those, you found yourself soaking wet with sweat. There were a number of occasions during the tour when people went down with heat exhaustion and medics had to put them on drips to right them. If you didn't have water with you, made sure you constantly hydrated yourself, that could easily be you.

From Shaibah, we were flown in a Hercules to Sparrow Hawk. This is literally just a runway in the middle of the desert, which was secured by vehicles. We flew in and got into the back of these empty Warriors to transfer us to Camp Abu Naji, our home for the next few months. I didn't see anything on that journey on the way into camp. The backs of those vehicles are pretty much all blacked out and we were straight into this dust bowl. The thing I do remember is that on the back bin of the Warrior there were a number of stripes. I asked someone what that was about.

'Oh, that's the number of militia they have killed.'

When we got there, the Light Infantry were preparing to leave. The usual drill is that the incoming regiment gets cross-contaminated with the one that is leaving. You have this handover where they show you the ropes, talk you through everything and then head off. The people doing the handover are usually desperate to leave, in this instance the Light Infantry had been there for six to seven months already. So they're tired and exhausted, but it is also when a unit is at its most professional. You want to finish your tour on a positive, making clear to the incoming soldiers what you have achieved.

But this tour handover was somewhat different. Such was the situation on the ground that rather than having the time for them to talk us through what was going on, we found ourselves thrown in from the off. We were fighting alongside them when we should have been chatting.

When we got there, the camp wasn't ready for the upsurge in action. Because the original assumption had been that this was a peacekeeping operation, the original sleeping and eating quarters were all tented and Portakabins. But the atmospherics had deteriorated to the point that the camp, rather than being safe, was at risk from mortar attack. Obviously a bit of canvas doesn't offer you much protection from that. To begin with, we would be sleeping anywhere that had a solid roof – offices, storerooms, corridors, workshops – and that added to the sense of chaos in the situation. They then brought in what were described as container huts, but they were essentially those big, rectangular containers that you see on the back of articulated lorries. They were sandbagged and were meant to have air con in but half the time those units didn't work. So they got really hot and honking: no windows, lots of flies, disgusting.

Eating also came with its risks. The kitchen and seating area were all tented, and it was a long walk around the camp to get there from the accommodation. Because of the mortar attacks, it was decided to stagger mealtimes, so that no more than 25 per cent of any company was allowed to eat at any one time. The flies were a problem here as well. To get anything down you had to master this technique of eating with one hand and waving the flies away with the other.

When it wasn't the flies or the heat, it was the dust. Abu Naji had a real problem with wind and it blew in the dust the whole time, caking everything in this thin layer. There were so many mortar attacks, the sirens were going off the whole time. They would continue long after the attack had begun, until the clearances were complete. If it wasn't the sirens, it would be some joker giving it the whistle, mimicking the sound of a mortar coming in, then everyone would start running for cover. And if it wasn't that, it was someone slamming shut the door of a Warrior. That sounded like a mortar going off in the distance. The whole place was jumpy, constantly on edge. I got a good sense of that as soon as I first stepped out of the Warrior.

If I was under any illusion about the challenge we faced, that soon went when we were attacked on 18 April, the first full day that our battle group had taken responsibility for the Maysan province. Camp Abu Naji was situated about 7 kilometres to the south of Al-Amarah, in the centre of which was CIMIC House, a FOB (forward operating base). Getting between the two always had the potential of being a risky venture. Al-Amarah was a town on the edge. A fortnight before we arrived, there had been a riot in the town involving about 3,000 people, stirred up by about 300 members of al-Sadr's Mahdi Army. Out of the three towns in the area, this was the crucial one; Majar al-Kabir and Al-Kahla had already fallen under al-Sadr's influence and had essentially been written off. Maintaining control in Al-Amarah, therefore, was crucial.

That day I was in the back of a Warrior, on a familiarisation patrol with some of the Light Infantry. There were three dismounts from the Light Infantry along with a commander, and three of us from the PWRR in there. The idea was that this was to be a routine patrol, where we would be taken to different spot codes, get out, have a look around and get our bearings, learn the landmarks. By spot codes I mean that Al-Amarah was divided up on the map into different colours and numbers – so one position would be Red 3, another Blue 5 and so forth.

We got to this particular point, Yellow 3, which was on the route into CIMIC House. Just as the door was opened for us to get out, the place exploded into a riot of noise. We had barely got out of the vehicle before the air was full of the boom and smoke of RPG fire and mortar attack. Wow. The attack was deafening and really concentrated. We were getting smashed so everyone dived back into the vehicle. We didn't return fire ourselves, but left it to the gunners in the Warrior to respond. I sat there in the darkness of the back of the vehicle, my heart thumping ten to the dozen, and listened to the battle exploding all around us.

'This is how it's been for the last two weeks,' the commander in the back of the Warrior explained.

We couldn't return fire ourselves because we hadn't been able to identify the firing point. In those brief few seconds squinting out into the daylight, I got a sense of just how difficult this task was going to be. Fighting in built-up areas, there were so many spots you could find yourself attacked from. It could be a rooftop, it could be a window, anywhere. Down on the ground, you were at a distinct disadvantage. That first attack was a real shock to the system, a wake-up call as to what the real situation was. I ended the day no wiser than I had been before as to the terrain I was facing. I just had the general sense of it being hostile, hard and unforgiving.

We quickly got into a routine of doing regular patrols. We were in rotation: a platoon out on the ground on patrol, another on 5 minutes' QRF, which meant 5 minutes' notice to move, and another on 20 minutes' notice to move. Only on the last rotation could your kit be off, your boots off. Otherwise, you were prepped and ready to go.

Out on the patrols, we'd do a lot of snap VCPs (vehicle checkpoints). We'd do that in a pair of Warriors: one would go at the front, the other at the back, so the vehicles had to work their way between the two Warriors and you had a bit of cover as you did your search. We'd do what was called a clean-to-dirty search on each chosen vehicle, clean being the inside of the vehicle and dirty the outside. We'd do a thorough search of the vehicle and search the individual too. That would be done on a rota, so every third or fourth vehicle, say, and then sometimes we'd mix that up. We'd be courteous to those we pulled over: '*As-Salaam Alaikum*, would you mind stepping out of the car?' But behind the politeness there was a clear message – we're here and we're in charge.

We'd get stuff thrown at us. They would throw stones and shit, which seemed to be part and parcel of the experience, kids thinking it was good crack. As soon as we set up a VCP, the kids would appear out of nowhere, asking for stuff, especially water. In a way, we didn't mind that as we reckoned if there were kids about then no one was going to try anything. It was when the kids weren't there that we started to worry that things were about to kick off.

There were a lot of attempts at hearts-and-minds stuff. Matt Maer was in the thick of that, trying to have meetings with local leaders, talk the situation through with them. We were given the task of trying to integrate and work alongside the newly formed local police force. We'd take them in and give them training at Abu Naji. We'd show them how to set up VCPs, how to spot something which was out of the ordinary. We tried to give them useful information without going into too much detail on our SOPs (standard operating procedures). A steer, essentially, on what was expected, without giving too much information away.

That was a show of faith on our part, a real attempt to engage with and support the local community. Unfortunately, people took advantage of that. The fact that we were inviting these guys into the camp to train them was potentially really dangerous. It meant they could get a clear grid of our camp, then go back to the mortar teams and tell them where everything was situated. By trying to be friendly to them it actually made things more deadly for us. And of course, that sense of being taken advantage of only served to erode trust between the two sides still further.

There's a phrase that did the rounds at the time that summed up the experience of being a soldier in these circumstances: Smile Shoot Smile. We were there to try and reassure and rebuild this community and you couldn't do that by being aggressive the whole time. But such was the strength of the insurgency that you couldn't turn the other cheek either. So you'd find yourself switching from a fire-fight back to shaking hands and smiling at kids and back again.

That was how we wanted to approach things. But the longer the tour went on, the harder that was to maintain. Friends of mine were getting hurt by the people you were expected to smile at. That made it difficult to carry on, for sure – a real test of your professionalism.

CHAPTER SIX

PIMLICO TO WATERLOO

BY THE START OF MAY, it was decided that a stronger response to the growing unrest and rising insurgency was needed. Getting ambushed was becoming a regular feature of going out on patrol and there was a real concern that Al-Amarah could go the same way as Majar al-Kabir and Al-Kahla. If they managed to take over Al-Amarah as well, that would mean withdrawing from our FOB at CIMIC House and essentially losing control of the whole province.

The consequence of all of this was the decision to take the fight to the insurgents. This resulted in a number of large-scale, set-piece operations, each named after a different station on the London Underground. The first of these, Pimlico, was slated for 1 May and was to be an attempt to arrest a number of the key insurgent players – a mixture of bomb-makers and Mahdi commanders. We'd got intel of the locations of a number of these and they were concentrated in the same residential area of the city: the Kadeem estate. The plan was to go in with a large show of force and capture them. A Company 1 PWRR had that task. C Company from the Royal Welch Fusiliers were tasked with controlling important junctions in the face of a counter-attack, while I was part of the QRF ready to go, back at camp.

The troops set off from Abu Naji at 02:00 hours. To begin, the arrests part of the operation went well. A Company went into the estate and were broadly successful in arresting the targets they had set out to secure. But as the troops withdrew, they came back under sustained and heavy fire. The Mahdi Army weren't going to let this incursion go without a response. By the time the prisoners were back and being processed at Abu Naji, the Mahdi Army's response was swift and forthright. Three members of the Iraqi police had been taken hostage and unless the detainees were released immediately, they would be killed. Meanwhile, all entrances to the city had been barricaded. To make matters worse, CIMIC House was revealed to be dangerously low on both food and ammunition. No one had thought to resupply the post before Pimlico had started. Now, supplies needed to get through and fast. If the Mahdi militia attacked CIMIC House, the soldiers there had next to nothing to fight back with.

That was where we came in. I was asked to change call signs and be a dismount commander for W20 (Whiskey two zero – the vehicle call sign) because they didn't have a commander. Having been ready to go in as QRF overnight, we were now assigned to head into town in broad daylight. I always say to people that I felt more scared that day than I did during the Battle of Danny Boy. That was because a lot of what was happening was out of my control. I was in the back of an armoured vehicle and at the mercy of events.

As we drove in, I could hear Second Lieutenant Richard Deane chatting to us over the intercom. He was our eyes as to what was happening. As we approached a point known as Blue 7, it was clear that our situation was starting to get serious.

'There's barricades,' he said. 'Burning tyres in the middle of the road.' I remember him pausing. 'This is a come-on,' he said.

At that point, all hell broke loose. The Warrior got absolutely smashed in a way I'd never experienced before: two missiles and a load of RPGs. It's difficult to be precise as to exactly what happened because of the wall of noise that exploded and ripped its way into the back of the Warrior. There was this blast of heat, a wave that smacked across me. One of the missiles had made its way through the thick armour of the Warrior and I could feel this burning sensation across my face and hair, my skin pricked and stabbed with shrapnel. It was difficult to see anything else, because the whole of the back was immediately full of thick smoke, but the stench of burning was really strong. I was coughing away. It was so confusing that for a second I wasn't even sure if I was dead or alive.

As the smoke started to clear a little, I could see Crucefix, one of the other soldiers in the back, who was sat opposite me. He'd got this big chunk of shrapnel embedded in his nose. Irvin, who was also in the back, had been hit in the leg and was going wild, with his LMG (light machine gun). He wanted to get out there and fight back.

'Mate,' I said. 'Can you hear it out there?' As the ringing of our ears from the explosions started to quieten down, the heavy noise of gunfire continued, rocking and shaking the vehicle. 'We're staying put,' I said.

Meanwhile, I could hear screaming. It was Sammy in the gun turret. 'I'm burning!' he was shouting. 'There's a fire. Someone help me!' I grabbed for the fire extinguisher that was situated above the back door. It was a different sort to the ones where you press a nozzle down and spray. Instead, you smash the bottom of it and throw it on to the fire. It sucks all the oxygen away from the fire and that puts it out. As soon as I smashed it, it instantly froze to my hand. I had to throw it off, feeling it rip my skin in the process. Being in that confined space meant that the extinguisher sucked away our oxygen as well. With that and the smoke I was finding it difficult to breathe. I got these rags and wetted them with water from our drinking bottles. The water was hot from being in the back of the vehicle but was the best I could do. I passed them round to everyone and told them to cover their faces with them. I was improvising. I remembered seeing something similar in the film *Backdraft* and reckoned it was worth a go.

Throughout all of this, I'd heard nothing from Deane and knew that he must have been hit. In fact, he'd been knocked out by the blast. Sammy, meanwhile, had got himself to Deane's rifle and was attempting to return fire to those who had attacked us. It was a desperate situation, the fact that they'd got through the vehicle's armour was frightening. Fucking hell, I thought. I'm not sure we're going to get out of this. I shouted to the driver, Johnson Beharry, (Bee) just to drive and get us out of there.

'Anywhere!' I shouted. 'Just get us the fuck away from the killing area!'

With a thump and lurch, Beharry took us forwards. There was an almighty smack and a shudder and I realised that he must have just driven us straight through the barricade that had been set up. The gunfire echoed on as we lurched forwards and the Warrior continued to shake. I kept tabs on the others in the back and as I did so I heard a sloshing sound coming from around my feet. Then I smelled it. I looked down and saw the floor of the Warrior was starting to fill with diesel. The tank must have been hit and the fuel was pouring in. It was like being driven around in a bomb. One spark of flame and the whole thing could go up.

I can't remember much of the journey to CIMIC House to be honest or quite how Beharry got us there. I know from accounts afterwards that we'd lost all communication with the rest of our company and that Beharry drove for much of the journey with his hatch open so that he could see out of the smoke that was still billowing out, which was incredibly dangerous given what we were facing. He also helped to get Richard Deane down from his turret before safely getting the Warrior into CIMIC House. It was outstanding bravery and he was rewarded with the Victoria Cross for his efforts.

I remember when we got there that the back of the Warrior was opened up by Steve Cornhill, a much more experienced soldier than me who I'd looked up to when I'd first joined. He opened the door and the look on his face told me everything I needed to know about how bad the situation was.

'What the fuck?' he said, before helping me to get the other dismounts out. I got Crucefix out and got him some treatment. The bit of shrapnel he had in his face from the rocket strike was the size of a credit card and he was bleeding quite badly. Eventually, one of the medics took me aside and had a look at me. I had a bit of shrapnel in my arm, a bit of metal. I thought I would be able to pluck it out, but the medic had a look at it and said that it was too deep and right into the bone and that I might need to go back to Shaibah, where the main medical centre was, and have it removed properly.

By now, the adrenaline that had been carrying me through the incident was starting to wear off a bit and I could begin to feel the sharpness of the pain from where I'd been hit. In particular, I was starting to get this pain in my eyes. It was a ripping sensation that was difficult to describe but basically felt as though I was blinking glass. My whole face had been pebble-dashed from the explosions, but it was my eyes that were worrying me. It was really starting to sting and I was having trouble seeing. I started to panic and was really worried that I was going blind.

'I can't see!' I told the medic, who tried to wash my eyes out with water, but it didn't seem to make any difference. I was struggling to keep my eyes open and they put a wet rag on my face to try and soothe it. The next thing I knew I was being wired up on to a drip.

We were taken back to Abu Naji in another Warrior and from there I was helicoptered back to Shaibah. I was in the hospital for four days while they ran me through a whole load of tests. The wait on those was nerve-wracking I can tell you. But the doctors did come back with good news. The tests showed that my irises had been badly scratched and I was suffering from blast burns but there was no permanent damage done to my eyesight. They made me wear this sort of medical blindfold to help my eyes recover, interspersed with regularly getting my eyes washed out. It was painful and irritating but I knew I'd been incredibly lucky and that the situation could have been so, so much worse.

Deane was there, in the bed next to mine. If I was lucky to be able to see, he was lucky to be alive. There were other serious casualties there as well – a platoon commander and another section commander. Everyone was really friendly and there was a great spirit and banter on that ward as we chatted through everything that had happened to us. The more we talked about everything, the more I was desperate to get back and rejoin the boys.

My spirits were lifted further when I received a surprise visit from a good friend of mine, Kev Marsh. Kev was also out on tour and was based over in Basra. He'd heard my zap number read out over the radio, so as soon as he could he commandeered a Warrior and drove over to see me.

'Mate,' he said, when he saw me. 'What happened to you, Cartoon Head?' Cartoon Head was a nickname he always used for me. 'Where has your hair gone?'

At this point, apart from being unable to see properly, I looked a right state. One of my nicknames in the army was Bearskin, because I've always had a good, thick head of hair. But the blast had burned off big chunks of it, so I had all these clumps missing. Kev gave me some grief for that.

'Come on,' he said. 'Let's get you out of here.'

The two of us went out to the NAAFI (Navy, Army and Air Force Institutes), a group that provides food, shops and restaurants for British troops. But the first thing I could smell when I got there was perfume. There were all of these girls going in, dressed up as though they were on a night out. That really shook me. I was there, still in my combats from the ambush, covered in dust and God knows what. My boots stank of diesel. I felt a right state, straight from the battlefield and these rear echelon soldiers didn't have a clue what it was like there out on the front line.

I was pissed off. 'I can't go in there,' I said to Kev.

Knowing what I knew about Al-Amarah, knowing what my mates were going through, I couldn't walk in there and act as though none of that was happening. It was funny. Sometimes I think that people back in the UK didn't really understand exactly what it was that we were going through, but it was shocking to discover that people down the road didn't get that either.

Slowly, day by day, my eyesight started to improve. I was desperate to return to the company. I took an eye test to see if I was ready, but I failed. I was determined to go back and so I asked to take the test again. This time, when I was meant to put my fingers across one eye, I just opened them out enough so that I could see. I don't know whether the doctor saw me do it. He knew I wasn't in any danger with my eyes. And so he signed me off and let me head back up north to rejoin the troops.

I had only been away from camp for a few days, but had already missed the next major operation. Knightsbridge took place on 3 May. This involved using a battle group, complete with tanks, to go in and resupply CIMIC House. The operation was successful, though the Mahdi take on the incident was not that they had been overawed by the use of tanks, but that they hadn't attacked the convoy because they had been asleep. So while the first aim of getting ammunition and food into CIMIC House was achieved, the second aim of making clear to the local population who was in control was not.

The result was Operation Waterloo, which took place on 8 May. Like Knightsbridge, this involved a resupply of CIMIC but this time, rather than getting in and getting out, the company would stay positioned at key junctions, inviting attack from the militia. If they engaged, then we'd be ready for them and meet them head on. If they didn't engage, then everyone would know they had bottled it.

Operation Waterloo involved the whole of C Company, so that's twelve Warriors, together with a further four Challenger 2 tanks. That's a big convoy, a real show of strength. We met up at Sparrow Hawk, the airstrip, and got ourselves into assault formation. At 02:00 hours, we started the rumble into town. The lights of the Iraqi National Guard camp flashed as we went past. Everyone knew we were coming.

Inside the Warrior, we were stacked full of rations to give to CIMIC House. Bacon, sausages, eggs, milk, even these gateau cakes for them to eat. We went past Red 11, which was one of the most dangerous junctions, and all was quiet. We drove on to Green 4, where there was a bridge you had to cross, to get on to CIMIC House. The tanks were too big to get over, so the plan was to manoeuvre them into position to secure the bridge, so they could offer cover for the advance on from there. Once the bridges were secure, the Warriors full of supplies would drive on to CIMIC and do the resupply.

We dismounted to check the bridge. I went out with one of the Fijians, Bruce, as a pair, primarily to have a look for wires, to make sure that the bridges didn't have any IEDs or anything attached. Suddenly, there was gunfire. We took cover and tried to return fire, work out where they had engaged us from. That's difficult enough, but especially in the dark. All you can see is people skipping from building to rooftop. They're never in position for a long period of time, so it's all but impossible to get a proper fix on them. All that you could do was to engage in the general direction of the gunmen who were shooting at you.

A shout came over the radio. Diff – Corporal Difford – had been hit. Originally it sounded as though he'd been hit in the throat, but it turned out he'd been hit in the foot. He was casevaced. Company Sergeant Major Falconer had a Warrior which had been turned into a sort of makeshift ambulance – the 'Millennium Falconer' – and he swept Diff up. Meanwhile, a message came over the radio to mount up. That was easier said than done. By this point we were about 100 metres away from our vehicles, with gunfire blasting away at us. Running back, you're really exposed. I ran, head down and as hard as I could, probably the fastest 100 metres I'd ever run. Luckily, I made it back.

We got over the bridge in the Warriors and drove on to CIMIC House. That was chaos. We remained under attack and just wanted to get the supplies over and get back. Remember, at this point the security of the Challenger battle tanks was sitting on the other side of the bridge. CIMIC House can only take a couple of Warriors, so those that could drove in and the rest of us were ordered to park up outside and throw the stuff over the walls.

That was mental. We were hurling it over. Between the gunfire we could hear it land with a thud and someone on the other side shouting *Cheers Mate!* The food was all flat-pack stuff on the whole, so it was basically okay. Though what happened to that gateau cake, God only knows.

Job done. We mounted up and drove back over the bridge, the convoy pulling up at Red 11. This was the real show of strength. Overlooking the junction was the OMS (Office of the Martyr Sadr), one of the main insurgent strongpoints. We got out of the vehicles and waited for the dust-up. It didn't take long to arrive. Before long, the night sky was lit up with tracer fire. It felt as though there were militia everywhere: on the rooftops, in the windows, out on the streets. We tried to take cover where we could and tried to engage. Every time they moved out, tried to get a shot, we would engage them and push back.

At one point, we got the order to get back into the vehicles and batten down. Someone had called in air support: an RAF Nimrod MR2 and an American AC-130 Spectre. Wow. I think that was the only time we had that sort of cover while we out there and it was an amazing thing to behold. They'd got a lock on some of the mortar teams we'd been fighting and blasted them. The explosions were enormous, the whole ground shook.

That intervention was decisive. It knocked the wind clean out of the militia. By dawn, the decision was taken to go into the OMS. One of the corporals who'd done an Arabic course shouted out over a loudhailer that we were coming in. A section was sent in to storm the building. It was empty of personnel – they'd all fled – but full of weaponry. The haul included mortars, rockets, bombs and mines, even a Russian automatic grenade launcher hidden in the library. Vehicles had to be brought in to carry the weaponry away. When they pulled up, an angry crowd had started to come together. But their complaints were interrupted by a low show of force fly-by from an RAF Tornado.

There was a real buzz about the place after Waterloo. It finally felt as though we were achieving, taking the fight to the Mahdi Army and asserting our control over Al-Amarah. Now the tour could kick on and begin to focus on the peacekeeping aspects that we'd originally been sent out to do.

That feeling lasted less than 24 hours. With no let-up in pace, we were back out on patrol the following day and in a convoy with a couple of other Warriors and a Challenger 2 tank. We were heading towards another junction, Blue 8, when there was a huge fireball. It wasn't us who had been hit, but one of the other Warriors. Sergeant Chris Broome gave a shout, then the intercom disconnected.

'What's happened?' I shouted.

'It's Lewy,' someone said. 'He's been hit. He's on fire.'

Lewy was Sergeant Adam Llewellyn, our Platoon Sergeant, who was in the vehicle in front. The man we all looked up to. A real operator. I dismounted and ran out to try and help. Fuck. Lewy's Warrior had been hit by a petrol bomb. Lewy was in the turret and had been consumed by the flames. Somehow he'd got out and extinguished himself. It was the most surreal, sickening sight. Stick was running there as well, with a fire extinguisher in hand. He used that to put the flames out on the vehicle, which was still on fire.

I ran over to where Lewy was. It's difficult to describe what a horrific sight it was. The skin was dripping off him, like melting off his body. Just this red, raw, steaming, burning flesh underneath. He was dripping all over the road. There were burns everywhere. His arms were a mess. His eyes were screwed shut and he was screaming – for water, for morphine, anything. The only water I had was hot, but I poured that on him and then tried to find his morphine.

Every soldier has their own morphine on them. It's your emergency supply for if, God forbid, something like this happened. It's meant for you and for your own use only. I crouched down to get Lewy's out of his pocket. But with his skin and everything, it was a mess and I couldn't get it out. Fuck it, I thought, grabbing for mine. That was against standard operating procedure, but he had to have it. I grabbed it out and put it in his leg.

We put the fire out on the Warrior then got Lewy into the back and tried to make him as comfortable as possible.

Then we drove on, to a police station, which was one of our locations, and tried to take stock. Lewy needed immediate medical attention and Stick was in a bad way, too, with breathing difficulties from smoke inhalation and fire-extinguisher fumes. So they were casevaced and the rest of us tried to take in what had happened.

There was a lot of upset and anger over what had happened to Lewy. He was the ultimate professional. I looked up to him. You wouldn't wish what had happened to him on anyone, but there was something specifically about it being him who had been hit that stuck with us. The strike rate of people being injured felt disconcertingly high. Diff the day before, now Lewy. It was difficult to shake the feeling, who was going to be hit next?

But what really, really stung was that the petrol bomb had been thrown by a child. A boy no older than ten. That was really hard to get your head round. How someone so young – just a kid – could do that much damage to a guy so big and professional as Lewy. How someone so young could be mixed up in this, could feel this way about us. Operation Waterloo had been meant to sort everything out. We'd done the show of strength thing and proved we could take on the Mahdi and win Their response had been to fight back like this, to respond by using a ten-year-old kid to get back at us. It was sickening.

When we were out on patrol, it had always been the kids who'd come and surrounded us. We'd been doing that hearts-and-minds stuff, shaking hands and handing out water to them. We'd done that, too, because as long as there were kids around, then we thought that no one would try anything and that we'd be safe. This attack, though, turned all of that on its head. Those kids could be as deadly as the gunmen we thought their presence was protecting us from. How could you trust anyone if a ten-year-old could be primed to kill you? How could these people, who we'd been sent out to protect and help, hate us so much?

That was hard. Really hard. My mind went back to the training I'd done before going to Kosovo, when we'd done exercises in crowd control. Those public-order exercises on Lydd ranges where you'd have rubber bullets fired at you and the other regiments would throw whatever they could at you, and as much as you wanted to go back and give them some, you had to stand there and take it, hold your discipline and shape. It felt a bit like that now. They'd shot Diff, they'd petrol-bombed Lewy and, man, part of you wanted to get out there and give them something back.

That was hard. Really hard. To hold all that in. We did, because we were the British Army and we stayed professional. But it didn't make it easy, for sure. Knowing that we had to go back out on the streets and face the people, see the kids running up to greet you, not knowing whether their smile of welcome was genuine or if there was a hatred of your presence, and the means to kill you, hiding behind it.

It felt as though the gloves were really off now.

And then came Danny Boy.

CHAPTER SEVEN

DANNY BOY

FOR ALL OUR ATTEMPTS to regain control of Al-Amarah, events elsewhere conspired to intensify the situation still further. In the days after Operation Waterloo and the petrol-bomb attack on Adam Llewellyn, US forces were involved in heavy fighting with supporters of Muqtada al-Sadr in the city of Najaf. Najaf is a holy city and is home to the Imam Ali shrine, the most sacred site of the Shia religion. Military action here carried a symbolic value that rippled through the rest of the country.

Having been attacked by al-Sadr's fighters, the Americans responded by moving their tanks into the centre of the city. There followed a battle in the city's vast cemetery, ironically called the Valley of Peace, about a mile away from the Imam Ali shrine. In the course of the fighting, the dome of the Imam Ali shrine was damaged, which al-Sadr's supporters immediately blamed on the Americans. The US denied this, saying that the al-Sadr fighters had caused the damage. But for all their protestations, the rumours spread like wildfire across Iraq. And at prayers on 14 May, imams loyal to al-Sadr whipped up anti-coalition fever. There was fighting in Nassiriya, where the coalition headquarters were attacked with RPGs, trapping staff inside. In Kerbala, a US forces complex was also attacked.

Back in Maysan province, the Mahdi responded with a double attack. In Al-Amarah, a patrol from CIMIC House was set upon. Orders rang out for forces to respond to that. Then came news that members of the A&SH (Argyll and Sutherland Highlanders) had been attacked close to a vehicle checkpoint known as Danny Boy. Danny Boy was on Route 6, south of Al-Amarah and a few miles from Majar al-Kabir.

Majar al-Kabir was a city with strong anti-coalition sentiment. This was to the point that a disputed agreement had been reached with the local population that British forces wouldn't enter the city. One year earlier, six members of the RMP had been cornered and subsequently killed by an angry mob. Given that previous history, and present-day accusations of holy sites being damaged, you had a tinderbox atmosphere ready to explode.

That day, 14 May, started like so many others, with a rocket attack at Abu Naji. We'd been on five minutes' notice to move when this attack came in. Such was the frequency of these attacks that you were almost prepared for them, took them in your stride. We were sent out in our Warrior to do a snap VCP, to try and see if we could stop and apprehend this mortar team. It was while we were doing this that word got through about the attack near checkpoint Danny Boy. That came from Major Adam Griffiths, commander of B Company of the A&SH. He'd been ambushed next to Danny Boy by what he estimated were ten men. His men had fired back and hit two, before they'd managed to escape from the ambush.

Griffiths and Stick – my commander – had an impromptu confab as to what to do. Then Stick shouted across at us to quickly collapse the VCP and mount up. Unaware that Griffiths had got through the ambush, Lieutenant James Passmore (PWRR), who was attached to the A&SH, had turned up to offer assistance. But with Griffiths gone, Passmore's men had found themselves pinned down and suffered two casualties. Our orders were to get to their location and extract them.

Before I knew it, we were heading down Route 6, getting ready to extract the casualties. The back of the Warrior, as always, was hot, dark, sticky, uncomfortable. Stick was giving me, Taylor and JC constant updates, what we were going to do when we got there when – BOOM! Out of nowhere the vehicle was hit by overwhelming firepower. The armour of a Warrior is thick but, as I knew from previous engagements, it is not impenetrable. The vehicle skidded to a halt as the ambush continued, rocking from the rat-a-tat of gunfire and boom of RPGs.

'Jesus, Stick!' I could hear Jean-Claude Fowler, the gunner, shout. 'Contact wait out.'

Stick issued a fire control order, then JC started to return fire, engaging the militia stronghold. We'd been shot so many times over the previous weeks, the fact that someone was firing at us didn't faze me. What was different, and what made me more concerned, was where we were being fired at from. It was normal for someone to take a potshot from a window or rooftop in Al-Amarah. It felt unusual for it to happen in the middle of nowhere.

Where the fuck were we? The only info I'd had was that we were going to extract two casualties. But this firefight was nowhere near our rendezvous. It was all a bit mixed up and confusing. Stick and JC continued communicating with each other while they tried to work out what was going on and how many enemy positions there were. All I could do was sit there, listening to the rounds spraying up against the vehicle. With a clunk I could hear the chain gun failing to fire, a 'Fuck' from JC and a grab for his LMG. He switched from using that on the turret to dropping down and firing the 30-millimetre cannon.

I kept my mouth shout. That's your job at that point. There's so much radio feed and the gunners really need to concentrate, so you have to give them that time, let them get on with it, rather than bombarding them with questions. Eventually, after what seemed like an age of being bombarded, I asked Stick what was going on. A stronghold, he told me. Looks like they were dug in. There were a lot of militia fighters – ten to fifteen, Stick estimated – and a load of weaponry around their position.

'Wait out,' Stick said.

The firefight continued. I sat there, poised, taking in the information Stick had just told me. Then I passed it on to the others in the back. *There's a stronghold. Ten to fifteen militia. We are engaging. Wait out, lads.*

'Woody,' Stick said, over the intercom. 'Prepare you and your men to dismount.'

Woah. Dismount?

'Say that again,' I said, as the engagement continued to boom away outside.

'I want you to prepare to dismount,' Stick repeated. 'We're not having any effect here. They're in these zigzag-type trench positions. Just popping up, engaging, getting down again. Let me know when you're ready.'

I'd been told. I explained Stick's command to the others in the back. They had the same 'what the fuck' response I had. You want us to go out into *that*? As I was telling them, I could feel my heart going ten to the dozen, smashing up against my body armour. Holy fuck, I was thinking. 'We need boots on the ground,' I told the boys. 'We're going to get out of this vehicle and launch a close-quarter counter-attack on to the stronghold, okay? Stand by and get ready to go.'

While they were prepping, I was talking back with Stick. 'What kind of weapons have they got?' I asked, though from the sounds hitting the Warrior, I had a reasonably good idea. 'RPGs? PKMs? AK-47s? It all sounds pretty punchy.'

'We'll support you,' Stick said. 'We'll be on rapid rate of fire before you open the door, so when you leave the vehicle, the enemy will have its head down and you can get out. There's a gully,' he continued. 'About ten o'clock. You'll see it straight away once you step out of the back door. If you go for that you'll get at least a bit of cover from there.'

I relayed all of this back to my dismounts. They were still looking at me as though I was mad.

'Lads,' I snapped. 'This is happening.'

At that point they tuned in, got their heads together, their kit prepped.

I took a deep breath. 'Stick,' I said, over the intercom. 'We're ready to go.'

'Okay,' he said. 'Stand by. H hour. Five, Four ...'

On the count of three, all hell opened up as JC and the gunner in the second Warrior blasted the stronghold for all they were worth. The door opened, I blinked and squinted in the brightness of the daylight. I didn't know where the trench was. I couldn't see it from where we were in the Warrior, with its one small window fogged up with condensation. The kickback from the gunfire was spraying sand and dust everywhere. All I knew was that I had to head to the gully at ten o'clock to try and give myself a chance.

I was pumped, could feel the adrenaline coursing through my body. In the back of the vehicle, I'd felt so many emotions, the biggest of them being fear, threatening to rip through my veins. I knew as soon as I started to feel that, I had to stop it and control it. Fear in that situation is contagious and I knew the other lads were looking at me. I needed to lead them out of the Warrior, so channelled that fear, turned it into focus for the challenge ahead.

I took one step on the sand and that was it. Once that foot was down I was fully committed. I was out of there. I just hoped that I wasn't going to be alone, that my dismounts were going to back me up and go with me.

Straight away, as soon as my eyes adjusted to the sunlight, I could see where I needed to go. I could see the cover that Stick had mentioned and I ran, as hard and as fast as I could. A beeline, straight for it, not stopping or pausing or even thinking about the gunfight going on around me. I remember reaching the cover and sliding in on my belt buckle. I heard noise and movement and there, peeling in next to me, were my dismounts. They'd followed me, made it across. It makes me proud thinking about that even now. I had to hold that in, though, compose myself and carry on.

'Are you okay?' I asked. They nodded yes. 'Right, take a breather,' I ordered. A cigar moment, I called these. Everyone was entitled to one. Pause, two, three, take the time to do your assessment of the situation. We'd got to this point of cover. The question thumping away in my brain was, What now? How do I get us out of here? There's three of us and possibly fifteen of them. Even with the covering fire from the Warriors, that's not great odds.

Now I noticed the noise. It was so loud, the rapid rate of fire that the Warriors were delivering. The second Warrior had its chain gun working and was firing over our heads. So loud, it was difficult to hear yourself think. But I needed to identify the enemy.

'I'm going to try to get eyes on,' I shouted to the others. And I did my meerkat thing, scouting back and forth, scouring the ground until I could identify them. Got you, I thought, looking dead ahead. I followed the line of rapid fire, the mud flicking up around the area that the Warriors were focused on. There was no sight of the enemy because of the gunfire, but I was sure that's where they were. There were clumps of gorse dotted around and I thought to myself, If I was the enemy looking for a position, that is exactly the sort of position I would go for, because it is great cover from view.

The stronghold was about 120 metres from where we were. How do we get there from here? I wondered. Tacking left felt exposed and we wouldn't have the cover from the Warriors. On the right, I wasn't sure what was on that flank. Which left going down the middle, hard and fast and aggressive, and straight up to that position. At that point, I saw movement in the trench. I looked up to see someone exchange fire with the Warrior, then saw a lot of bobbing heads. My heart was in my mouth. I wasn't sure we stood much of a chance, really. But I couldn't tell that to the guys I was leading.

I heard a noise behind us. Joining us on the ground were Corporal Mark Byles and Private Beggs – Beggsy. They must have come out from the second Warrior, though I wasn't paying attention to what was going on behind me. And because my radio seemed to have packed up, I wasn't in comms with anyone to let me know what was going on.

Byles was the senior commander, but I'd been on the ground longer. I told him what I'd seen and observed and what I thought we should do. He did his estimate and agreed. We decided to work in two fire teams, Charlie fire team and Delta fire team. I took charge of Delta fire team, commanding Rushy and Spud. We'd move in stages, leapfrogging each other forwards: once we engaged, the others would move past us, start to engage and then we'd move forwards again. It's called the leap frog method and was something we'd practised during our exercises, but never out in the open like this.

I checked my radio again. It was fucked. I couldn't report back to Stick and tell him what we were doing and I wouldn't be able to talk to Byles either, once we started. It was going to have to be old school – hand signals and shouting, a bit of luck and hoping for the best. I looked across at Tatawaqa and Rushforth and gave them the nod.

'Stand by,' I said. 'Right. Let's go!'

The three of us scrambled up and ran. We hard-targeted, by which I mean that we zigzagged towards the enemy position, making it more difficult to be shot. From those first few steps, we were completely exposed. I knew the enemy had seen us. Once they engaged, we were down on a knee and returning fire – the cue for Byles and Beggsy to move.

I was waiting for the cry 'Man down!' Was expecting it, dreading it any second. But it didn't come and instead I shouted to move forwards and the three of us were in another bound. As we went from position to position, I could feel my confidence start to grow. Fuck me, we might actually *do* this. Against the odds, we might actually pull this off. The distance came down: 120 metres became 100, became 75. We got to 50 metres from the trench and I could see some of the militia leaving their positions. That was a real boost – that they saw us coming towards them and made to cut and run.

Looking back, I'm so proud of my men. When you think about it, what we were doing there was crazy, running across open ground towards a trench full of militia. That was courageous, bordering on foolhardy. Any of us could have got shot at any moment. It was going over the top, First World War-type stuff, a world away from the urban fighting we'd done on the rest of the tour. That and the lack of radios, it was almost old-fashioned, timeless stuff. Exactly as the British Army had fought down the centuries: a combination of courage and hope. The fact that none of us were killed is remarkable, really.

At the time, I wasn't thinking about any of that. I wasn't even that sure what the other fire team were doing. I was so fixated on the direct threat. In tune with the battle, pushing to keep the battle rhythm going and keeping the aggression up high.

We continued to leap frog with Charlie fire team. When they fired, we moved. When we fired, they moved. Step by step, we got closer to the trench. Bzz bzz bzz. The shots were zipping past, like bees buzzing around your ears, the rounds not too far away now. By the time we got to 25 metres away, you could see their faces. They were full of expressions of surprise, which spurred me on further. They clearly hadn't expected us to be that aggressive, to take the fight to them in that way and to have got anything like as far as we'd got.

The battle was shifting over in our direction. There were men down in the trench. Others were withdrawing, getting out and making a run for it. The numericals started to tip towards us. We were no longer outnumbered in the way we had been earlier.

Fifteen metres. I was close now and could see the look of fear in what was left of the militia. Five of us bearing down on them. Unscathed from everything they had thrown at us. I was gearing up to go in when, in that last split second, they threw their weapons down and put their hands in the air. That throws you. You're so focused on going in, to switch from one extreme to another is a bit like slamming the brakes on. You've got to snap into ceasefire and arrest and detainee mode, when your body is still pumping, the adrenaline from the firefight still pulsing through.

It sounds strange, but it's really hard. These people have just been trying to kill you. Shooting away at you, trying to take your life and then, like a flick of a switch, they have their hands in the air. To be a soldier running across open ground like that, it's like an out-of-body experience. You are possessed. You've got all this anger and aggression and adrenaline to control, you have to put a lid on it and get into arrest mode.

'Get the fuck down!' I shouted. 'I want hands in the fucking air. NOW.'

One of the militia was quite animated. His hands were moving all around. He was jumpy and unclear and I wasn't sure why. Was he nervous? Was he signalling? Was he about to try something? I wanted him away from the weapons systems, where he was no longer a danger.

At this point, we were in the trench properly. There were a number of bodies. Militia who'd been shot, who from their injuries and wounds were clearly dead. But I didn't notice them at this stage, as I was focused on this guy, he was the threat I had to deal with. So I carried on talking with my weapon pointed at him, stepped over the bodies to get to him. I needed to get to him and move the weapons away, reducing him as a threat.

But as I got to his position, that hazy lull in the firefighting was shattered by another hail of gunfire. I had no idea where it was coming from, but my immediate response was to grab the militia fighter and pull us both to the ground, before either of us got shot. I had a second reason for getting him down too, in that I didn't want him moving for one of the weapons that were lying there in the trench. So it was a grab on the shoulder and a shove down, firm but essentially well meant.

I was worried. We'd got to the trench, but the shooting was still continuing. I didn't know whether that was more militia or the ones who'd left the trench setting up elsewhere and continuing the fight from a new position. It was a confused situation in the trench as the bullets were flying. There were bodies, there were prisoners, there were weapons. I got panicked that one of the militia who was still alive might grab a rifle and spray us. I shouted across to Rushforth to get the weapons, collect them up and get them out the way. I'd never been in such close-quarter combat like this before and was doing my best under the circumstances. Everyone was doing their drills – my men were doing ours, Byles and Beggs were doing theirs. It was one of those situations when you realise just how valuable your training is. It's all stored away, like muscle memory, kicking in when you need it. My overriding priority was the safety of my men. I wanted to make sure that no harm could be done to us in the trench and that's what I focused on. But it was a confusing situation, as I say, a lot of shouting, a lot of gunfire overhead, a lot of tension and uncertainty.

Byles shouted over that we needed to segregate the enemy dead and the POWs (prisoners of war). At this point we got our plasticuffs out to cuff the POWs, put blindfolds over their eyes. While we were doing this, Byles went off with Beggs and carried out another close-quarter engagement. Meanwhile, more British troops had arrived on the scene – two further Warriors and a couple of Challenger battle tanks. Among the new arrivals was Company Sergeant Major Dave Falconer. He came over, along with Stick, to assess the situation. Stick was great – very calm, coordinating a lot of what needed to happen with the POWs and enemy weapons. I was glad of his presence.

The CSM (company sergeant major) came over to me, took one look at the trench and said, 'Fucking hell. What's happened here?' I gave him an outline summary, as best I could, as to what had just happened.

'Okay,' he nodded. 'And is the battlefield clear?'

That was a huge integrity question for me. Because for a split second, I really wanted to say yes. I really did not want to experience again what I had just been through. I felt that I was lucky to be alive. But clearly, I couldn't say yes when I knew that it wasn't.

'No,' I said. 'It's not clear, Sir. When we were approaching the trench, I saw a number of militia leave and fall back from this position.'

Falconer didn't even blink. 'Right,' he said. 'Fresh magazine on. You are going to take me to where they went. We need to do a clearance patrol.'

CHAPTER EIGHT

LOOKING FOR BRAVO ONE

A CLEARANCE PATROL. Fucking hell. That did *not* sound a good prospect. But Falconer was one of the most inspirational leaders of men that I ever worked closely with. His presence, his conduct, the way he delivers himself, he's outstanding. If I was going to pick anyone to go and do pairs fire and manoeuvring with, it would be him. So while I did think, You are joking me, when he said we were going to do it, at least I'd be doing it with him.

The two of us pepper-potted along the left-hand side of the main position that had been cleared: 20 metres, 50 metres, 80 metres beyond. We scanned the area, scanned our arcs for any sign of movement. Nothing. Dry fire and manoeuvre we call it. Unlike when we approached the trench, we didn't need to offer covering fire because at this point we couldn't see the enemy. You were primed to do so if needed. The person not moving would have their weapon ready, one foot planted on the ground, watching and observing, eyes open for any sign of the enemy.

'Target left!'

After 80 metres of clearing the area to the front, a militia fighter appeared as if out of nowhere. Down in another ditch, hiding, he popped up with his weapon raised. As soon as he saw him, Falconer put a number of rounds into his chest.

'Target down!' Falconer shouted. 'Move!'

As I moved another bound, another fighter stood up, no more than 10 metres away. I dropped to my kneeling position and engaged. The fighter was so close that when I hit him, I could hear him coughing and struggling to breathe his last gasp of air as he crumpled to the ground. I can still hear that noise now. But back then, there was no time to think.

'Good drills!' Falconer shouted. 'Move!'

We bounded on. We were about 120 metres away from the main trench position and pretty isolated. 'Sir,' I said, 'it's only you and me out here. We are really vulnerable.'

'Right you are,' Falconer said, scanning around. 'I think it is clear now, but we should get back. We'll do another sweep with the vehicles.'

We started to head back towards the main trench. Still bounding, still dry fire and manoeuvring. As we did so, I saw something flicker in my peripheral vision. Fuck, I thought, what's that? I spun round with my weapon raised and there, again as if out of nowhere, right close to me, were two more militia men. This time, though, they stood up, with their arms in the air. I shouted at them to put their hands up, which they were doing, and they were speaking back at us in Arabic. I didn't understand, but the gist of what they were saying, that they were surrendering, was clear.

As I was walking towards them and got closer I had to double-blink. There was something going off in my memory and then I realised that I recognised one of these guys. He was in the Iraqi Police force. He was one of the policemen we'd taken into Abu Naji for training and mentoring. I looked at him and he stared back. He knew I knew exactly who he was.

'What the fuck are you doing?' I shouted at him. 'Fucking hell.' I turned back round to Falconer. 'We had this guy going through training and mentoring. He's fucking betrayed us.' I turned back round to him. 'You fucking cunt,' I shouted. I was fuming with him, proper pissed off. He just stood there and smirked, like he didn't give a shit.

We didn't have any plasticuffs with us, so we had to put one arm behind their back, then walked them across to the main trench position. One of the guys was wearing these sort of flip-flop sandal things and as we walked over they kept coming off. Falconer, who'd been relatively calm up to this point, stopped the guy and said, 'If that flip-flop comes off again, you're not going to have any more flip-flops.' It wasn't just that it was irritating, we couldn't be completely sure that he wasn't trying it on, deliberately trying to slow us down while we were still exposed. Anyway, sure enough, this guy's flip-flop came off again. At which point Falconer picked up the flip-flop and hurled it across the desert. 'Right,' he said, 'now fucking walk.' And we frogmarched him back barefoot to the main trench.

By the time we got back to the trench, things had moved on. Army medics had arrived and I could see one giving one of the militia fighters CPR. Another of the militia was sat down, on a drip, with a field dressing on his left leg where it looked like he had been shot. His condition didn't look life-threatening – the medic had done his work and stabilised him. We handed over the POWs to Stick, I think, to sort and I sat down to rest.

I was properly exhausted. Mentally, physically drained. I remember sitting on a bank and having a drink of water to try and compose myself to carry on. The adrenaline you get from that sort of incident, it really carries you through, but the moment it is over you feel this huge crash and that's what I was going through. It's a bit of a cliché talking about a roller coaster of emotions, but that lurching up and down was exactly what it was like.

It couldn't have been for long, resting up, before the sergeant major came over. 'Woody,' he said. 'We need to go and collect these bodies in.'

'Say again, Sir?' I said. 'We need to do what?'

'We've got to collect the bodies,' he repeated. 'The call has come through from brigade. They think that Bravo One might be among the fighters.'

Bravo One was the name we'd given to the main militia leader. If he'd been apprehended or killed, that would be a big deal. Gathering the bodies and returning them to camp for identification purposes was an unusual request. That wasn't what we normally did. But such was the importance of working out if this individual had been part of the battle, that this was what was decided needed to be done.

It was a horrific task. There were a lot of bodies and they were seriously messed up from the gun battle. The bodies were heavy, even when a few of us were carrying, and they were covered in blood, wounds exposed. At first we didn't want to make skin-to-skin contact with the bodies and tried to carry them by their clothes, their cuffs, but the clothing was all loose and started to come off. So we just had to grab them. Some of the bodies were so disfigured, opened up, that you had to be so careful just to try and keep the parts intact. Horrible, horrible details that really lodged firm in my headspace.

Some of them were really young, that's what I remember thinking. We were talking 17, 18 years old. Kids really. I knew that if we hadn't killed them, they would have killed us, but even so. Having fought these individuals, gone through the battle, then looking at the bodies afterwards, it was brutal. To take another person's life is a lot to process. To pick up that body afterwards, it makes what you've done hang heavy on your shoulders. I wouldn't wish that upon my worst enemy.

Out of everything that happened that afternoon, this was the part that I have struggled with the most. In those days, months and years ahead, this was the memory that would come back to me repeatedly. It's what would come out at me when I was least expecting it, what I'd dream about, wake up in the night with a rush. I hated being made to do that.

The vehicles were moved down, so it wasn't as far to carry them. But, frankly, it was far enough – there were plenty of bodies to move. When you stepped back and looked at the number of militia involved, the weapons captured, it did strike you how big the incident was that we'd just been through. This wasn't some off-the-cuff attack. It was a full-scale ambush. Once again, I found myself thinking, How on earth did we get through this without receiving any casualties?

Because of the need to get the bodies back to camp, we didn't go back to Abu Naji in our normal Warriors. Two of the Warriors were assigned for the bodies, and the others for the POWs and the rest of us to go back in. You obviously did not want to contaminate the living with the dead. I can't remember whose Warrior I went back in, but it wasn't my own. We were all squeezed together, sat on two benches opposite each other. There was a Fijian lad, but not my dismount, Tatawaqa, who went back in a different vehicle. A guy from 9 Platoon, I think he was there. And various POWs.

It was pretty much silent in the back. No one was saying anything, everyone just lost in the dark in their thoughts, the pulsing heat of the afternoon, the rumble of the engine. I remember at one point, one of the Challenger tanks broke down. So we all had to stop and wait for that. We opened the back door to let some air in, but no one got out. That was a wait. We had to sit there until the recovery vehicle turned up. Given everything that had happened, we couldn't just leave the Challenger on its own, sitting there.

We drove on. One of the militia opposite me started to pucker his lips. Didn't say anything but the puckering was enough to be understood: he wanted some water. By this point, we were pretty down on supplies. I had very little water left, which, as it had been in the back of the Warrior, was boiling hot. But after everything we'd been through, I thought, No way, mate. My priority is my men. That water is being saved in case they need it. I knew that it wasn't going to be long before we were back at camp. So he could wait until we got back there before he had anything, I thought.

The day was getting on by the time we got back to camp. The temperature had dropped a few degrees and it was dark. When we got to the main gates, there was a lot of commotion. The gate lights, these big spotlights, were all lit and there were people all around, shouting and pointing. The commander of the Warrior I was in told me to dismount and go to the front of the gate. When I got there, the Provos (Provost) were waiting for me. They're an internal sort of regimental police the Provost sergeant and Provost corporal were there to make sure that discipline remained intact.

The Warrior I was in with the POWs headed off elsewhere in the camp where they were processed. Meanwhile, I walked up to the Regimental Aid Post (RAP) to help Stick,

Taylor, Rushy and JC with the unloading of the eight enemy bodies which were in my vehicle W22.

When I got to the RAP, which was all floodlit, there was an army doctor waiting for us. He told us what we needed to do with the bodies, getting them out and laying them on to the body bags. Those were all laid out, in a strip on the side. We went round to the back of the Warrior to open the back door. The door is opened on a sort of hydraulic ram: you press the button, the power kicks in and the hydraulic ram pushes the armoured door open. It needs a kick like that because it is so heavy, you can open it manually from the inside but it takes time and effort.

We went to open the door. I can't remember who pushed the button, but when they did so, nothing happened. The power had gone.

'Fuck,' they said. 'So what do we do now?'

As if this day hadn't been bad enough. 'You're not going to like this,' I replied. 'The only way to open that is for someone to crawl down through the turret, climb over the dead bodies and open the door manually from inside.'

We looked at each other. None of us wanted to do that. Even from outside the vehicle you could smell the stench of the bodies. Even after the Warrior was hosed down later on, it would still stink for weeks – the blood, faeces and fat oozing down into every crevice.

'Okay,' I said, 'we're going to have to draw for it.' Taylor, the driver, lost and had to do it. He was a big guy, bent nose, the sort not to be fazed by anything, but I could see he was nervous. And that was fair enough, frankly. It was a fucked-up thing he had to do. As he prepared to go in, he turned to me and the other lads and said, 'Can you talk me through as I'm climbing down?'

We watched him go in and make his way down and into the back of the Warrior. He got to the door, where he started to hand-crank it open. There's this sort of super-sized Allen key that you turn and as Taylor did so, and the door started to inch open, the rest of us outside recoiled as the stench from the bodies hit us. I was talking Taylor through – 'You're doing great, mate, that's it, keep it going, almost done' – and the door continued to widen. Then, well, I'm not quite sure what was happening, because out of nowhere, Taylor started shouting. He was shoving for the door and pushing himself out.

'He's alive!' he shouted, barging past us and running off.

Rushforth, who was there with me, was staring in. 'One's alive in there!' he shouted. With this, some of the medical staff came running over to the Warrior. Rushy then said, 'They're all fucking dead' and started laughing. It was his attempt at black humour – an attempt to help Taylor by releasing the tension.

The doctor came over, fuming with Rushy. 'What is going on?' he asked.

As we looked in, we could see that one of the bodies, which had been flat, was now sitting bolt upright and looking out of the vehicle at us. He was clearly dead but, God knows how, he was sat upright.

The doctor handed out surgical gloves, and with the help of the medical staff we started to carry the bodies out on to the bags. I'm not sure that rigor mortis had started to set in, but they were pretty stiff now as well as being heavy. There was all this white stuff oozing out and all over you. I didn't even know what that was and didn't want to find out. As we lowered them down on to the bags, the doctor was going round and labelling them up. Once all the bodies were out, one of the guys undid the access plates underneath the Warrior. We'd do that after most journeys, as there'd have been so much stuff about – usually lubes getting split and diesel and stuff like that so you'd get the access plates and let them drain clear. This time we did it and – woah – all this blood and fat and God knows what poured out on to the ground. It was disgusting and smelled completely honking.

Once those were drained, we took the vehicle round to the dust bowl, which was the name we gave to the vehicle park, which was where we cleaned the vehicles. That was when the medics came over and offered to help. Fair play to those guys.

'You've been through a lot,' one of them said. 'We will help you clean the vehicle.'

So they got stuck in with disinfecting them. I was told to go off and have a shower. One of the medics looked at my kit, which was by this point covered in blood.

'You'll need to bag that up and take it to the incinerator,' he said. 'And we'll need to test you as well.' That happened a couple of days later, when I was told there was a small possibility I might have contracted hepatitis B and was given a course of injections.

I wandered over to the showers in a daze. Showering at the best of times in Abu Naji was a risky business, with mortar rounds and stuff coming in, but to be honest I was so tired by this point I wouldn't have noticed. The showers were in this Portakabin, so I got in, stripped and leaned against the wall and the plastic sheeting as the water showered me down. I could see this mixture of blood and sand and grit washing off me and swirling its way down the plughole and I just stood there, dazed, and tried to make sense of everything that had happened to me on this most fucked up of days.

CHAPTER NINE

RED EIGHT

NORMALLY AFTER A PATROL, you have what is called an after-action review. But because the aftermath of Danny Boy rattled on into the night, that just didn't happen. There was some sort of wash-up the next day, but it wasn't with everyone involved as people were back out doing their next patrols and different tasks. One of the priorities was returning the bodies of the dead militia soldiers to their families. Under Muslim tradition, burial usually takes place within a day or so after death, so those needed to be handed back. They were driven out to an agreed place where they were passed over.

So some people got on with that. And we went back out on patrol. I remember going back to the vehicle the next day, opening the back and all these flies flew out, followed by this smell of flesh. For all the cleaning, there were still stains all over the seats and seat belts, the canvas pockets where you stored stuff were all smeared with blood. We were still finding bits of dried blood clots and body fat under the flooring plates for days afterwards.

You couldn't escape the aftermath of the battle, even if you wanted to. But we didn't speak about it properly. I think that everyone was in agreement that it was just a pretty fucked-up day. The details, the ins and outs of what happened, we didn't really go through with each other. It was kind of done. We moved on and braced ourselves for the backlash that we were expecting to follow.

A couple of days later, the RMP arrived to take statements from everyone about what happened at Danny Boy. That was all quite cack-handedly done. We were still on routine and when they appeared to talk to me I was on immediate QRF on five minutes' notice to move. So I did my statement in a room there, in the QRF room, with one eye on the clock the whole time. It wasn't very thorough. I guess they'd obviously heard a lot about the battle by the time they got to me and had seen the state of all of us as well. I think they understood the nature of that tour and, as a result, gave us a bit of leeway in the questioning rather than really grilling us.

At the time, that was fine by me. It just felt like a bit of admin to get done and the quicker I could get through and rejoin the boys the better. Looking back, it would have been much better for everyone concerned if they had been more rigorous in their approach. That might have saved everyone a lot of grief and hassle. But no one was thinking in that way at the time. It was more job done, on with the next.

In fact, the weeks after Danny Boy were something of a comparative lull. It had been such a high-octane few weeks with that and operations such as Pimlico and Waterloo that what followed was relatively calm. The attacks still came but they tended to be more isolated and more opportunistic. The mortar attacks would still come, especially when we were in Al-Amarah, but they weren't sustained in the same way: a potshot, then silence. So we were never able to fix a position and engage in response. Resupplying CIMIC House became easier. Waterloo and Danny Boy, it seemed, had knocked the stuffing out of them.

I didn't talk about Danny Boy with the other guys. And I didn't talk about it with Lucy when I was writing or ringing home. You'd get these 20-minute cards to make a call, but with sat phones the signal was so intermittent that you rarely got all your time. And even when you did get through, you'd have all this echo back and forth: *Hello? Can you hear me? I can hear you, can you hear me?* And so on, like you were speaking from the moon. I couldn't talk about what I'd been up to with Lucy. The line wasn't secure and for operational reasons you never went into details. It was always a weird conversation. They knew what was going on, or the broad thrust of it, from seeing the news; you knew what was happening because you were there. But because you couldn't talk about it, you had this chat as though nothing was really happening.

In a way, it was easier with my dad and my brother because they had a better sense of what I was going through. I still wouldn't go into details with Dad, but he knew from what he'd read and how I spoke that we were in a situation.

He wouldn't talk specifics but would offer me reassurance and support. He'd always sign his letters off the same way: 'Stay low, move fast'. Great advice! My brother, he was with 1 SCOTS who were serving in Northern Ireland. We didn't communicate as often, but he was an infantry soldier, like me. So he understood the tempo.

The only time I did speak to Lucy about what was going on, I regretted it. I gave her a call when I was in hospital after Pimlico. I rang and told her that I had been involved in an incident. *I am fine*, I said, *because I am on the phone to you now. I am injured but I am recovering. That's all you need to know.* The call was meant to reassure her, but by having to leave it vague, I'm not really sure how much that helped. I think it only makes you worry more.

I was aware, too, of the pressure that Lucy was under at home. She was a new mum, dealing with a newborn baby while her husband was away. That's enough of a burden by itself, without hearing about him getting smashed up every single day. In a funny kind of way, I suspect Lucy was behaving the same towards me. If she was having difficulties with Bailey, she wasn't going to let on because she didn't want me to worry while I was out there. We're kind of similar in that way, which is probably why we get on so well. We were both being stretched in our particular circumstances, but tried to stay resilient and positive when speaking to each other, even when we felt the opposite.

*

Two weeks after Danny Boy, it was my platoon's turn to do our stint at Broadmoor. Broadmoor was the nickname we gave to the Iraqi prison that we used as a forward operating base halfway between Al-Amarah and Camp Abu Naji. It was here that we were deployed as a QRF. Because of its location, it meant that we could halve the time it took for us to respond to any incident. Everybody took their turn there – three days on, then back to camp again.

Such was the ferocity of the tour, that there was plenty to respond to. In army terms, it was one of the noisiest in recent history – the noisiest since Korea according to some accounts. That didn't stop, even when you got back to camp. I remember coming back from one battle in town and heading back to camp to grab some food before carrying on. The cookhouse was a bit of a walk, at the far end of camp, so you were always a bit vulnerable there at the best of times. As usual, the wind at Abu Naji was doing its swirling trick of covering everything with dust. As usual, too, the flies were everywhere. They were determined to get your food.

I had been there once with Sergeant Adam Llewellyn before his incident and there was such a hurry we barely had time to wash our hands and dry them with that evaporating alcohol gel the whole cookhouse seemed to stink of. On this occasion, we didn't have time to eat in the couple of tents that served as the canteen. It was just grab some food and run back for the next round of action.

As Adam and I were heading back for the vehicle, we heard that familiar whistling sound. Mortars. Incoming. Every time you heard it, there was that split second lurch inside you, it was such pot luck whether they landed safely out of harm's way or whether this time it was your turn. BOOM. The thin, high-pitched whistling sound gave way to the dark thuds as the mortars were hitting home. This was a serious spanking the camp was taking. Adam and I were exposed out in the open. Down went the food as we dived for the nearest cover, which in this case was underneath a Portakabin. It was a brief respite and I remember lying there and the two of us laughing at the ridiculousness of the situation. Fragments were flying everywhere; the food we were desperate for a forgotten memory.

'This isn't safe,' Adam shouted at me, above the noise of the explosions. 'If one of those mortars hits the hut, we're going to become casualties. We need to get back to the Warrior.'

The Warriors were hard cover. On Adam's count we made a run for it, full speed back to the vehicle. If a mortar had hit us at that moment, we would have been done for. But we made it back and in, sat there in the back catching our breath. All the while outside, the now muffled thud of the mortars continued. We looked at each other and started to laugh.

'So much for lunch,' Adam said.

'Fuck.' My stomach twinged at the thought of food. I knew we were going to have to get back out there having had nothing to eat. Those flies who'd been following us would be dining out on our meals or what was left of them among the explosions and the dust.

Compared to Camp Abu Naji, Broadmoor was a strange place. Moody. Atmospheric. Eerie. There's something about being in a disused prison, particularly at night, that tends to make you jumpy. There wasn't much light and it was a big, echoey space. We were rattling around in there, just ten or so of us sleeping in. In a strange way, the cells were the most comforting place to be. That's partly because they were cool. Such was the Iraqi heat that we'd sleep directly on the floor, to allow the chill from the brickwork to seep into our sweaty bodies. But the cells were a good place, too, because they were secure. With the rumble of mortar attacks ever present in the distance, it was a safer place to be than in the tents back at camp.

As usual, when it was our turn to be the QRF, we were sat around waiting for the call. Some of the lads would play cards – 21 or poker were the favourites, but I've never been that good, so I wouldn't take part. I'd be there reading a book or a magazine, joining in the banter about home, about footy, about the situations we'd been involved in on the ground. All the while it reinforced us as a unit, which made what was about to happen next all that bit harder.

The prison was so big that one of the lads acted as a runner, to relay news from the Ops Room back to us. On this evening, I can't remember whose turn it was, but he came piling over with the news for us to head out. Camp Abu Naji was getting spanked, more than the normal mortaring, they had been receiving really heavy incoming fire for effect. If we were quick, we had a chance of catching that mortar team as they made their way back into the city. We had a location. Our mission was to find, fix and destroy.

It was late. Dark. A pitch-black, moonless night as we drove out of Broadmoor and towards Al-Amarah. We were in two Warriors – I was in W22, Whisky Two Two, with Stick – who had been with us at Danny Boy. The other warrior, W20, was being driven by Johnson 'Bee' Beharry and was under the command of Second Lieutenant Deane.

We drove into the city in darkness, with no lights on. To begin with there were street lights on, guiding our way, but pretty soon they went off too. The first thought was that it was a faulty generator again – electricity cuts and blackouts were fairly standard. But the situation was more sinister than that. It was actually another come-on. The mortar team knew exactly what they were doing, drawing us in and waiting.

We knew that the mortar attack had been fired from somewhere within a grid square, the corners of which we called Red Eight, Purple Four, Red Nine and Purple Three. We were coming up towards Red Eight when there was an almighty explosion. Something had been hit. A hail of fire rained down from the rooftops. In the back of the Warrior, I was shouting, asking what was going on. But there was so much gunfire it completely disorientated everyone. We were getting smashed from the rooftops and it was impossible to get a fix. I could hear Stick shouting, too, radioing the other Warrior to see if they were okay.

We started to manoeuvre, jockeying as we call it, where the vehicle shimmies forwards and back, so it wasn't standing still, a fixed target.

'Fucking hell!' Stick suddenly shouted. 'The boss's wagon has taken a direct hit. Two of them. Direct to the turret.'

He radioed them again. No answer.

'What about the vehicle?' I asked. 'Is there any movement?'

'None.'

This did not look good. There were no heads in the turrets. At best, they had battened down; at worst, well, it didn't bear thinking about.

'Fuck it,' Stick said. 'We're going to back it up.'

At this point, we were about 50 metres away from the other vehicle. Under Stick's instructions, we reversed up so our vehicle was directly in front of theirs. I knew exactly what was coming next.

'Woody!' Stick shouted. 'I want you and Coops to step out. Go on up to the top deck and see what is happening.'

'Sure,' I said. I turned to Coops – Private Cooper – who was sat next to me. 'We're going to jump out. Go and have a look.'

Coops was cool. 'No worries,' he nodded. 'Let's go.'

As soon as the back of the Warrior opened, the noise ratcheted right up. Inside the vehicle the sound of gunfire and mortar was all muffled. Out in the open, it was deafening, disorientating. With the street lights out, the only real light was from the tracers coming from the AK-47s. That and the sparks flying from the bullets hitting the vehicles: the ting-ting-ting as they hit the framework was incessant.

I tried to focus in, to get my bearings as quickly as I could. The open door of our vehicle gave us some protection from gunfire. But not much. I knew that we had to be quick because the longer we were out there, it was only a matter of time before a bullet hit home.

I looked into the driver's hatch and immediately the reason why the vehicle wasn't moving was clear. There was blood everywhere. Bee was sat there, completely out of it, big gashes all over his head where he'd been struck. The hit had come through the hatch. An RPG, it had exploded about a foot from his face. He'd got hit so bad that the shrapnel went into his skull.

'Bee?' I shouted, trying to get a response. But there was nothing. I checked his pulse. He was alive, just about. But little more than that. I knew at that point we had to get him out of there. At a stroke, the mission had changed. The mortar team we'd been sent to take out were forgotten. Now it was all about getting Bee back to Broadmoor as quickly as we could.

It sounds strange with bullets flying around, but I wasn't really worried about my own safety. I was too concentrated on Bee and just how we were going to get him out. We undid the seat belt and Coops and I grabbed his arms and dragged him out, carried him over to the back of our vehicle.

'Someone is going to need to drive that Warrior back to the Broadmoor,' I said. I assumed that was going to be me, but Coops stepped up to do it. Turned out that a few weeks before the incident, Bee had taken the privates for a lesson in how to drive the vehicle, so they'd know what to do in precisely this situation. I was a trained driver, but Coops was insistent.

'Bee showed me how to drive a couple of weeks ago,' he said. 'I'm all over this.'

'Okay,' I said. 'Look, just follow us. If there is any issue, I'll take over.'

With that, we drove off. Bee was flat out on the floor of the Warrior. I talked to him, chatted away in the hope he'd respond, but there was nothing. Back at Broadmoor, word had got out about our situation and a helicopter was already being scrambled to take Bee off for treatment. We screeched back, straight through the sangars – the sentry posts at the front. Coops, who'd driven perfectly behind us up to then, got a crash course in how big his vehicle was. Rather than driving between the sangars, he took one clean out. Luckily, the lad on sangar duty was okay.

The helicopter came down and we loaded Bee on to it. It wasn't nice seeing him like that. But it was good to see that the response had been so quick. We stood back and watched as the helicopter rose up into the night and with a whup-whup-whup it whisked him away for treatment. And that was the last time I saw him for a long while. In fact, I wouldn't see him again until the ceremony at Buckingham Palace, where he was awarded the Victoria Cross and I got my Military Cross. He still had a scar from the incident, from where they picked out all the fragmentation.

Bee wasn't the only person to have been hit. Richard Deane, my platoon commander, had been hit again, this time just beneath the eye. He had a laceration that was pissing with blood. Thankfully, it looked worse than it was – just a nick really.

I remember feeling really gutted afterwards when the helicopter went off. Up to that point, I was so hyped up trying to get a response and doing what I could to keep him alive I hadn't had time to think. Now, though, all I could think was, Fucking hell. Another one. Another guy who was a great asset to the company, taken away from us.

There was no way any of us were going to get any sleep after the incident, not with the adrenaline still pumping through. So we sat up, talking through the incident, tried to get it out of our systems. But it didn't work for me. When I did decide to finally call it a night, I went back to the cell where I was sleeping and kicked the cot bed in anger. Booted it again and again, trying and failing to get my frustration and anger out.

CHAPTER TEN

COMING HOME

I CAME BACK from the tour of Iraq early. There was a section commander battle course I was earmarked for, so I returned home to Tidworth advanced, ahead of my regiment. There was no decompression for me, no stretch of days unwinding with the lads before going back. Instead, I was straight back to see Lucy and Bailey, my five-month-old son who I'd barely seen. That was exciting. I'd missed them both and couldn't wait to see them. I didn't have long with them before I had to head over to Brecon to take the course, so wanted to make the most of it.

As soon as I got home, however, something wasn't right. And that something was me. I thought we'd be back playing happy families, but the reality was something different. Bailey, my beautiful little boy, he didn't know who I was. Those precious first few months of his life, that all-important bonding time, I hadn't been around for. Now I was back and he was like, Who's this guy? I desperately tried to get to know him, but he responded to my touch by crying and could only be calmed down by his mother.

I wanted to be a father to him, but all I was was a stranger he didn't want to know. That hurt. It cut me up inside something rotten. And I felt this anger too. Frustration with the situation, a rage bubbling under that threatened to burst at any moment. I felt like I was on a crash course of learning to be a father and failing miserably. Everything I did was wrong. Lucy, bless her, tried to be patient, to explain what I should do. I knew I should listen to her, that she had had six months of bringing Bailey up and understood his every need and whim. But rather than helping, that just wound me up even more. I couldn't take it out on Bailey, so I took my frustration out on her instead.

On one occasion, we were talking about feeding. Lucy was trying to explain to me how to make up a bottle, the temperature it needed to be and so on. It was an ongoing list of instructions, how to do it exactly the way Bailey liked and in the end I just snapped. I threw the baby bottle smack against the wall. It smashed, causing milk and formula to run down the paintwork towards the floor.

'Fuck you then,' I shouted. 'You do it.' Lucy tried to calm me down, but I was having none of it. 'Bollocks. Not interested.'

It wasn't just over Bailey we were clashing. Lucy had had the house to herself for months and had got herself into a routine with her newborn. That can't have been easy bringing him up on her own, but she was resilient, stuck at it. Now I was back, I would leave my kit around the house. My combat boots here, my daysack there. Lucy, who'd had the house neat and tidy for my return, would ask me to put things away. That also pissed me off and I would respond in an aggressive manner.

'If you want the bag moving, you fucking move it,' I told her. 'Don't tell me to move my bag.'

I would constantly put her down, what she was wearing, what she was eating, nitpicking at everything she did. Hurting her feelings seemed to be a daily occurrence.

'Are you trying to test my patience now?' I roared at her in one discussion, about putting my socks in the laundry bin. 'Have you any idea what I've been through? This shit, it just doesn't matter.'

Lucy didn't know what I'd been through in Iraq. And I didn't really know what I'd been through either, not really. Not in a way I could communicate or discuss with her. And because I didn't talk about it, it sat there, within me. And it bubbled up in the form of rage and anger. It wasn't me, both of us knew that. How I was acting wasn't like I'd behaved before I left for Iraq. And it didn't just manifest itself as anger. Frustration, envy, jealousy all poured out of me. Lucy was an incredible mum, I could see that, but rather than being pleased or proud of her, the better she was, the more it pissed me off. Because I felt that I could do just as well at being a dad, but Bailey didn't want to know. It stung. And what made it worse was that Lucy stood by me. She didn't argue or fight back, but tried to manage my anger. But that just made it worse.

*

After five days of this of trying and failing to cope, I got a phone call from Sergeant Major Spicer.

'Woody,' he said, 'how are you doing?'

'Great,' I said, lying through my teeth. 'It's going really well.'

'Listen, I hate to interrupt you on your family time, but I've got some really sad news. It's Chris Rayment. He's been killed.'

I took that like a blow to the stomach. Ray was a good guy, young like me, a real life-and-soul type, always full of humour and optimism. He was a big Charlton Athletic fan, wouldn't shut up about them, had always been there with a bit of banter about football and what have you. Hearing the news back in my own house it felt like the war was creeping into my life even here. I couldn't get away from it.

'How did he die?' I asked.

This in a way was the worst bit. Ray hadn't been killed in battle. His death was a tragic accident. He'd been at CIMIC House and one of the vehicles that was leaving got caught up in a wire, which brought the security barrier down. It slammed right down on top of him. It was just awful. You survive everything the militia can throw at you and then you die like that? The guy was just 22. It was heartbreaking hearing the news. An absolute bloody waste.

'We're going to have to repatriate him,' the sergeant major explained. 'I want you in the repatriation party, to be there when they bring his body back.'

Ray was going to get a full military funeral. In total, there were seven of us, six carrying the coffin and the sergeant major leading the procession, the driver to give him his proper name. This meant rehearsals – two days in Tidworth and then on to RAF Brize Norton. We'd do some more brush drills there, then meet the Herc coming in. We'd bring the coffin off the plane, load it on to the hearse and then head to the chapel of rest. It was a difficult thing to do, no question, but in a strange way I was glad to be asked. It meant I got out of the house and got back to the world I knew.

It was a cool summer's day as I stood at RAF Brize Norton, watched the Herc do a circle of the base before coming in to land. It parked up and then the tail came down. We marched on, the six of us, two ranks of three and up to where the coffin was. That was an awful moment, seeing it there draped in a Union Jack. I had to give myself a real talking-to: You owe it to Ray to give him the best send-off you can. The Union Jack didn't go all the way over the coffin, just up to where the plaque was, with his name on. Don't look at it, I thought. Just don't look at it. Of course, I looked at it. I read the brass plaque, Ray's name, the dates and could feel myself starting to go.

'Take a moment, boys,' the sergeant major said. 'Compose yourselves.'

I was grateful for his intervention. Did that blinking-back thing. Tried to clear my head. Come on, Woody, get a grip. What would Ray say if he saw you like this now?

One of the RAF air crew pulled the Union Jack fully over the coffin.

'Prepare to lift,' the sergeant major said.

That was it. I clicked into action, into the routine we'd practised. In unison, the six of us put our hands under the coffin. I was at the middle, on the right-hand side. Under the sergeant major's command, we lifted in unison, up and on to our shoulders. They're heavy things, coffins. If you've ever carried one, you'll know. Heavy twice over. We did a right turn and then started to slow march, carefully, respectfully, down the ramp, on to the tarmac below. The journey across to the hearse felt as though it took for ever. We could see the black of the vehicle glinting in the sunshine. Could hear Ray's family: the crying, the wailing, as we got closer. I had to blank that out, stare off into someplace else, otherwise I would have gone myself.

Once the coffin was in the hearse we joined the procession as it headed into London. We stopped at a cadets' centre, where Ray had been trained, had a minute's silence then went on to the chapel of rest. The next day, we collected Ray and headed on to the church for the funeral itself. Outside in the graveyard where he was buried, a ceremonial row of soldiers and weapons waited, ready to give him a 21-gun salute. At the end, as the coffin was laid out, there's a routine with taking off the Union Jack. This gets folded up into triangles, the last one tucked in, then the medals and headdress are placed on top and handed over by one of the coffin bearers to the deceased's relatives. This was done by the CSM. Once the last post was finished, he walked over, stiffly, awkwardly, to Ray's mother. It was heartbreaking to witness.

It was such a long day. It was extremely late by the time we got back to Tidworth. I was absolutely physically and emotionally drained. Back at home, you could cut the tension with a knife. Lucy didn't know what to say. I didn't know how to talk about what I'd been through. She left me alone, gave me some space, which was probably the right thing to do. But at the time, the flash of anger bubbled up from within again. You're not even asking me how I'm feeling, I thought.

Ray's was the first military funeral I'd been to. Five days later, I went to my second. This time it was Lee O'Callaghan, killed in an attack on his vehicle by insurgents. Lee was only 20. He was football mad – supported Millwall FC and was good to kick a ball round with as well. Because we'd been drilled already, I got the phone call from the sergeant major and went through the whole thing again. Lee's funeral was huge. He was from a big Catholic family and the church was packed out.

On the way to the service, we stopped off at The Den, the home of Millwall FC. Dennis Wise, the club manager at the time, and Theo Paphitis, the owner, were both there. They gave us a wreath and a football shirt and then there was a minute's silence outside the ground. Once again, it was an energy-sapping day. Really took it out of me. Back home that evening, I was sat in the dark again, staring at the wall. To go from that back into normal family life, it just didn't work.

I felt guilty, that I was alive and Ray and Lee were dead. But more than that, I couldn't shake the feeling that it could have been me. On top of everything I'd been through it was a lot to process and to be frank, as a 23-year-old, I didn't really have the tools to do it. Not that help was offered at the time, by the army, but even if it had been available I wouldn't have had the nous to ask for it. I am a soldier, I thought. I will deal with it myself. It's not right to go and talk to anyone. That's not what we do.

In a selfish way, I was glad when it was time go to Wales for my course. I went back to being a soldier again. And it was something else to think about, to focus on and take my mind away from the dark thoughts that continued to percolate within me.

Certainly, I had to have my shit together for the course. The section commanders' battle course is known as being one of the most difficult in the army. Four and a half months long, it's training you up to be tactically sound in the field. You learn how to analyse the enemy, and to be an instructor in most British weapons systems. You learn how to be a leader, to command men into battle. So it was half weapons instruction, half tactics. It was career progression stuff, was linked to promotion. And you had to have your head screwed on to get through it.

For me, it was exactly what I needed. I could bury myself in the work, rather than thinking about the difficulties of family life. Staying in Brecon, being back among the day-to-day of living with soldiers, that had the familiarity I craved. A home away from home, in a strange way. I didn't have time to mull over what I'd been through in Iraq. Could park those dark thoughts for now and get on with my life. Or at least, that's what I thought.

One day, not long into the course, I was giving a lesson on the rifle. We were taking it in turns to instruct each other on the course. There was a knock on the door and two men walked in. They were in civilian rather than army clothes, suited up and were from the SIB (Special Investigations Branch).

'We're looking for Lance Corporal Brian Wood,' one of the men said.

'What's this about?' the instructor asked.

'I'm afraid we can't discuss that here. We need to take him away for an interview.'

I stood up. All eyes were looking at me. Inside, my mind was racing. What on earth were the SIB doing here? What did they want with me? As I followed them out of the room, as they led me out of the building to an office in the camp down the road, I felt sure there must have been some mistake. I didn't feel so much worried as pissed off. Here I was knuckling down, on a careers course. I didn't need these sort of distractions.

The SIB officers took me into an office and sat me down in front of a computer. Suddenly, it all felt quite formal and serious.

'We need to talk you about the Battle of Danny Boy,' one of the officers said. He pulled a folder out of his bag. I recognised the document, my handwriting. It was my statement of what happened that day.

'There are just a few discrepancies that we need to clear up.'

We sat there and went through what I'd written. At one point in the statement, I'd written that there were four prisoners taken back in the Warrior. At another, I said there were three.

'Can you explain that?' the officer asked.

There were various answers to that. It was a typo. I was tired. The events had come so thick and fast I couldn't remember everything and had recollected as best I could. I wasn't quite sure where the questions were leading, but there was nothing more to it than that.

The SIB officers, however, seemed to think differently.

'We're going to show you some photos,' they said. 'Of the prisoners of war that were taken that day. We'd like you to tell us which ones you recognise.'

Really? I thought. I could tell them straight off the bat that I wasn't going to remember who was who. As we flicked through the photos on the screen, there was only one of the detainees who I recognised. He was a bigger, chubbier guy and the reason I knew him was that he was the one who had originally been an Iraqi policeman. We'd trained him up and then he'd gone and switched sides.

'I appreciate this might be distressing,' the officer said, 'but we also need you to look at the pictures of the Iraqis who were killed and see who you can identify.'

This was now not only pointless, but upsetting. The photos were grim – bodies from the battlefield with appalling injuries. Sat there in the army office in Brecon, it brought it all back. I was being sucked back into Danny Boy, just as I was trying to get over it. I wasn't going to erase those images from my mind for a long time. I did what they asked, looked at each photo and for each said I didn't recognise them.

This went on for about an hour. Then I went back to the lesson and tried to carry on. When I got back, the instructor asked me what it was about. I told him they wanted to ask me questions about one of the incidents in Iraq but I didn't elaborate beyond that. I was annoyed. I couldn't see the urgency, why I had to be pulled out of the lesson in that way. It definitely did affect my emotions and focus on that course. The course is designed to promote you to gain an extra rank, it's demanding mentally and physically, so to play with my emotions I thought was unfair. They'd have known the course at the Infantry Battle School was one of the hardest.

The questioning wasn't aggressive. It felt more bizarre and random. I couldn't understand why I'd been pulled out of a lesson to be sat in front of a computer. They wanted me to give them answers I couldn't give because I couldn't remember what the dead looked like or because it wasn't true or I couldn't remember. There were no accusations at that time, not directly. But there must have been someone saying something somewhere. They wouldn't have asked me questions on my statement otherwise. Some suggestion of mistreatment must have come from somewhere. They must have done it for a reason.

Looking back, this was the start of it. The lighting of the long fuse that was to slow burn under my life until it exploded into accusations and the full glare of a public inquiry.

CHAPTER ELEVEN

PRIDE AND PTSD

WHEN IT WAS announced that I'd been awarded the Military Cross, I must confess that I was so naive, I didn't even know what a citation was. I certainly didn't know that anyone had written a citation about my own actions. So when it transpired I was going to be awarded the medal, it took me completely by surprise.

That announcement took place in March 2005. Following on from my tour in Iraq, my next posting had been in Germany, Barker Barracks at Paderborn. It was there that our commanding officer called a scale A, which is a parade that everybody has to attend. As we crammed into the large theatre there, rumours whipped round as to what the parade might be about. It's not very often that you get an event of that size, so we knew we were going to get some important information. The word from those who seemed to know about these things was that maybe we were about to be moved back to the UK.

Lt Colonel Maer took to the stage. Almost a year and a half earlier, he had stood in front of us at the gymnasium in Tidworth and told us that we were about to embark on a tour like no other. This speech, in a way, was the opposite bookend to that. Maer spoke about the tour and what we had achieved out there. Then he announced that the operational honours list for the tour had been announced and that a number of members of our regiment had been honoured.

The first name on the list was Johnson Beharry, who was awarded the Victoria Cross (VC) for his actions in Iraq. He was the first member of the PWRR to be awarded the honour and one of only a handful of living people to hold that honour (at the time of writing, there are just nine living VC winners). His VC was announced to huge applause. Lt Colonel Maer announced that he and Major Coote were both going to be awarded the Distinguished Service Order (DSO) and that Stick, Sergeant Chris Broome, was going to receive the Conspicuous Gallantry Cross (CGC).

Maer, Coote, Broome and Beharry, it later transpired, were among those who'd already known about their awards. They'd been over in London the previous day, to be told about their honours and to speak to the press in advance of the announcement. All of them had been sworn to secrecy, so that the parade in Paderborn remained a surprise. Back in Germany, the list of achievements went on. The number of soldiers from the regiment who had been mentioned in despatches was as long as my arm: Crucefix was on that list, along with Passmore.

But the regiment had also received a number of Military Crosses. The Military Cross was first awarded in 1914 and was originally given to soldiers of the rank of captain or lower, but that distinction was abolished in 1993. It is awarded for 'gallantry during active operations against the enemy'. The regiment had been awarded a handful, among them Corporal Byles, CSM Falconer, Second Lieutenant Deane and ...

'... Lance Corporal Brian Wood,' Maer announced.

Wow. I was so surprised when he read my name out, to begin with I thought I must have misheard him. I'd been sat listening to all the names being awarded and thinking to myself, this is brilliant. It was such a difficult tour and it's great that the army are recognising this and rewarding us. But when my name was read out, it was difficult to take in. I was just a young lance corporal. I didn't know about these things. And certainly, no one had talked to me about such a possibility.

Later on, I got hold of my citation, well, a copy of it anyway. I still don't quite know how I got it. I presume Second Lieutenant Deane and Stick must have sent something, that went up to Major Coote and things happened from there. The citation itself is on a serious-looking form. 'ASI Subject to Confidentiality' it reads across the top. 'Restricted – Honours' it says underneath. Then there in block capitals was my name: 'LANCE CORPORAL WOOD'. The citation then went through three specific incidents for which I was being awarded: the attack on the Warrior during the aftermath of Operation Pimlico on 1 May, when I had to put the fire out in the back and was hit by shrapnel;

secondly, the events at Danny Boy on 14 May; and thirdly, on 11 June, when I'd helped to save Johnson Beharry after a direct hit by an RPG.

On the first incident, I was described as showing 'exemplary leadership' and worked 'with no regard to his injuries'. During the Battle of Danny Boy, it said 'his level headed leadership and swift, courageous action were an inspiration to his men and an example of text book infantry tactics employed in the face of numerically superior and heavily armed enemy.' Of the ambush at Red Eight on 11 June, it said 'dismounted in the face of sustained and accurate incoming enemy fire to extract the wounded.' The citation concluded by saying

Each one of Lance Corporal Wood's actions deserve credit in their own right; his performance on the 1st May prevented further injury to his colleagues and arguably saved their lives. His leadership, courageous and selfless acts on the 14th May and 11th June, despite previous injury and in the face of continued enemy fire, were an example to his men. He has demonstrated the highest virtues of a young Junior Non-Commissioned Officer and is worthy of the highest public recognition.

After my name was read out, people were cheering and applauding. I had all sorts of emotions going on. It was nice to be recognised but I also found myself feeling guilty too, that I'd been chosen for the honour but Tatawaqa, Rushy and Beggs weren't mentioned. That didn't seem right. Without their actions, I wouldn't have achieved what I wanted to achieve. I know how hard the CIMIC House soldiers fought and there were only a few decorations within that company. But where do you draw the line? In my opinion, there should have been other people awarded gallantry medals. But of course you receive it with pride and wear it with pride.

It was great recognition for the regiment and I wear the medal for the others as well as myself. When I told Lucy I'd got the award, she couldn't believe it. Then it was out on the honours and awards list and my phone went mental. That was a lovely moment, all of these messages pouring in. It was very humbling how many people were pleased for me.

The investiture ceremony took place at Buckingham Palace a couple of months later. I took Lucy and my mum and dad. The day before, in one of those odd moments, I'd been in a music studio recording some music. A while previously I'd been on one of the army football tours to Mauritius. There'd been this band called the Dooley Brothers and someone had got the guitars out and we'd had this singalong. Anyway, someone suggested that when we were back in London we recorded a song. It was called 'Shadow Bay' and was about a soldier leaving to go to war. After everything I'd been through, it felt like an opportunity to have a laugh, so I'd agreed. This Mercedes pulled up outside my

My granddad Robert Patrick Wood, Highland Light Infantry, India 1930–7.

My dad, Gavin Wood, second right in the front row with his nine brothers. They served in the Royal Highland Fusiliers and the Highland Light Infantry – I come from a very military family.

School photo with my notorious hair.

First family holiday, Tunisia 1991.

Winning the county
cup final with
Hampshire.

The ultimate leader. Adam Llewellyn days before being hit by a petrol bomb thrown off a rooftop by a child.

Hearts and minds was an important aspect in Iraq, but you couldn't let your guard down because of what happened to Lewy.

The Warrior's small back window that was full of condensation and sand.

The Warrior on the Sparrow Hawk runway outside Camp Abu Naji.

Private Rushforth heads towards the Warrior away from the burnt-out battlefield.

1 May 2004: Johnson Beharry VC carrying his helmet that was hit by a 7.62mm bullet, which penetrated his helmet and remained lodged on its inner surface.

14 May 2004: Battle of Danny Boy. After three hours of fighting we had the final enemy position cleared. AK47s, RPGs and militia fighting equipment all on show.

18 March 2005: Buckingham Palace, receiving the Military Cross from Queen Elizabeth II.

Proud parents and wife outside Buckingham Palace.

On patrol led by
4 Platoon B Company
1 PWRR. Nahr-E Saraj,
Helmand,
Afghanistan 2012.

Returning home to
my family after
Afghanistan, my final
military tour.

Carrying Lee O'Callaghan who was killed in action in Iraq.

Rehydrating my friend and double amputee Jay Baldwin during our epic 3,000 mile bike ride across America.

End of the trail at the finish line at Santa Monica Pier with all the team.

house and took me to the studio. Nothing ever came of it, but it was a good experience and great fun.

My dad was a bit wound up about it. He is army through and through and needs a timeline and a structure, so when I said I was going off to do this recording, he wasn't happy. The following day, we had an argument on the way to Buckingham Palace. I was in full uniform service dress and my dad was driving us from the hotel. We were rammed into this tiny black Vauxhall Corsa. It's never the most relaxed experience driving in central London and my dad's quite a fiery stress head so he was moaning away. We were all probably a bit tense, it was a big day after all, but I was telling him to stop moaning and get out of the bus lane and so we started arguing.

'You fucking drive then!'

'Fucking hell, I'll drive then. Pull over.'

The car screeched to a halt and with horns blaring around us we got out and swapped seats. I had my full kit on as I said and my big ammo boots, which all made the Corsa feel a bit like a toy car. We eventually got to Buckingham Palace, only to be told that we'd gone to the wrong gate and then had to drive around again until we found the main gate to the palace. But once we parked up, all that was quickly forgotten. My dad was all choked up as we walked through the Buckingham Palace gates.

'I'm five foot eleven, son,' he said to me, 'but today I'm sixteen foot five. I'm so proud of you.'

We walked into a lobby area, where a marshal directed the friends and family to go one way and take their place in the seats to watch, and those who were receiving awards were ushered into this holding area. I say holding area, but this was Buckingham Palace rather than a military camp, so surroundings were somewhat grander. There was a whole mixture of people getting their awards: Johnson Beharry was there to receive his VC, as well as a number of the recipients from my regiment. But there were people who'd done amazing things for charity, sportspeople, all sorts. Ellen MacArthur was there, who was being made a dame. Sir General Mike Jackson was receiving another award. It was all very surreal, chatting to all these people. It was great, too, to talk to Johnson. Because he'd been away getting medical treatment our paths hadn't crossed. This was the first time we'd chatted since I'd pulled him out of that vehicle. There was a real mutual respect for what we'd done for each other. He'd saved my life, and Coops and I had saved his.

The ushers told us how the ceremony would work. We were funnelled through into the main hall, going in one by one to receive our awards. There was a line on the carpet we had to walk up to, then you turned to your left and walked up to the first step. The Queen would be there, stood on the second step, and she'd pin the medal on you. As I went through in the line to wait, one of the ushers looked at me and said, 'Hello, Brian'. I realised it was one of my dad's friends, a pipe major from the Royal Highland Fusiliers.

'I used to babysit you when you were knee-high,' he said. 'Now look at you. I'm so proud.'

The wait seemed to go on for ever before I was called to get my medal. But then my name was read out and the usher told me to go in. The hall where the medals were being awarded was huge and there was this big crowd of people watching, but to be honest, I didn't really take any of that in or notice where Lucy and my parents were. I was super-nervous and concentrating real hard on not doing anything stupid like falling over or making a fool of myself in front of the Queen.

When I got to the step, the Queen spoke briefly to me as she awarded me my medal. She said to me that it was so rare for her to hand out these awards for bravery. As she pinned the medal on my chest, she told me to wear it with pride. And I promised that I would.

There's a line that Winston Churchill once said about such awards. 'A medal glitters but it also casts a shadow,' he said. Afterwards, we went to a reception party, which was put on by the regiment. I remember holding Johnson's VC, seeing his name and number on the back in gold writing. That was kind of cool, but at the same time I wouldn't have wanted everything that went with winning such an award. That's quite a burden to carry around. It becomes your life and you can easily find yourself pulled from pillar to post. I think it took a while for Johnson to learn to live with that.

Some people are funny, too, about such awards. Most people are just happy for you, but there were people in the regiment who were resentful that I'd been rewarded and not them. That's true of other people, too, even relatives who have never once congratulated me. One person said, 'Oh, Military Crosses, they give loads of them away', as though what I'd got was nothing. So the flip side of this public acknowledgement was this bit of jealousy or bitterness from others – that it should have been them up there, not me.

Everyone is different. It would be easy to get carried away with such an award, but I've never tried to live off my decoration. I was a soldier and enjoyed doing that and as far as I was concerned I just wanted to carry on as before and didn't make a big deal of it. I don't like speaking about the medal, even now. It's a great thing to have, but there's a lot of history behind it, a lot of memories that accompany that achievement that I don't like to think about. So the medal lives in its pouch with my others, locked away. And apart from Remembrance Day and specific occasions, that's where it stays.

When I came back from Iraq, I didn't know what PTSD (post-traumatic stress disorder) was. Didn't have a clue. It wasn't something that was brought up or discussed in terms of what we'd experienced in Iraq, or how we should handle it afterwards. Maybe I missed some of that because I came home early from the tour, but I don't think that was the case. It just wasn't a topic that came up.

How they would have done that, I don't know. In a military atmosphere, in a male-dominated environment, it's difficult to get anyone to open up. And that is particularly true for anyone who is a commander or a decision-maker. If anyone had come up and asked me if I was okay, I'd have probably told them to fuck off. I'd have seen that as questioning my ability and I'd have pushed back. I was young and considered myself fit and robust. To admit to having doubts and concerns, I'd have seen that as weakness and reckoned that others would have seen it that way too. I was young and ambitious. I wanted to get promoted. So any thoughts I had that way, I kept them to myself. But memories arc like scabs. It's very easy to scratch at one, to open up those wounds and thoughts and emotions. Those moments when you are quiet, alone, it's very easy for them to pop back up and for you to quickly go down a rabbit hole with what you remember.

I didn't speak to many people about what I'd been through. Not with Lucy, who I didn't think would understand from not having been there and also because I wanted to protect her. I spoke to my dad and my brother, but not in great detail, even though they might have given me sound advice having got where I was coming from, having both served themselves. But we didn't have that sort of relationship where we talked about those sort of things in that way. I didn't talk about it with the other guys in the regiment. We'd all been through it, we knew what it had been like, we all in our different ways wanted to move on. So I kept a lid on it and thought I was doing a pretty good job of doing so.

I couldn't hoodwink everyone, though. Sue, Lucy's mother, she saw through it. She said to Lucy, *Brian's changed*. She could see it in the way I was. Before I went to Iraq, I'd always been known as this happy guy, this bit of a jester-type character. Afterwards, as much as I thought I could switch it back on, I'd lost a bit of that somehow. I tried to joke, but it was more forced than for real.

And my patience, too, that had definitely gone. I was angry and short-tempered, particularly with Lucy. Never physically, but verbally I would go for her. I could get pretty nasty with what I said. I came out with all sorts and it just wasn't me, who I was really like. But I would snap her head off. With Bailey, he'd be crying as every baby does, and I couldn't deal with it. Didn't have the patience to calm him down. So I'd hand him over to Lucy and walk before I did anything stupid, anything I'd regret.

The nights were the worst. Bailey would cry and then I would wake and wouldn't be able to get back to sleep. I'd get up, sit there on the sofa in the dark and find myself staring into space, thinking about it all. It was a sort of deep daydreaming state I got myself into. I'd be back on the battlefield, running through everything that had happened. I could be down there for hours, before I'd snap out of it and head back to bed.

The bodies. I thought about that a lot. The collection of the bodies from the battlefield at Danny Boy and carrying them, loading up the Warriors. The smell of them, the weight of them, the feel of carrying these lifeless men into the back of the vehicle. And that guy that the CSM and me had shot when we were clearing the battlefield. The other one who'd been in the gully 10 metres away and who I could hear choking for his last breath. I could hear that sound vividly, echoing around in my head. I couldn't get away from it, even if I wanted to. The questioning by the RMP, the funerals, the Military Cross – every couple of months there seemed to be something else that brought it all back and those nights on the sofa all started up again.

I got offered a place to go and teach recruits at the Infantry Training Centre in Catterick. That was a big honour. It's the gold standard of instruction in army terms and as a young junior NCO it was an offer that was difficult to turn down. With my experiences in Iraq, particular at Danny Boy, I was the right fit. The fact that I'd won the Military Cross, too, meant that there was probably a bit of a poster boy element to it as well. Here's Woody, he's been there and done that, he's been honoured for it. So I found myself talking about what I'd been through, instructing on how to fight in close quarters, in hand-to-hand combat.

It was a real kudos thing to do, going to Catterick. But on a number of levels, it was a mistake to have done it. As much as I really enjoyed the teaching and instructing, the last thing I needed, looking back, was a job where I was being made to talk about and go back through those experiences in Iraq. It was a mistake, too, in terms of me and Lucy. All the pressures we'd had since I'd come back from tour, what I was going through and dealing with a young baby, they were piling up. Catterick, for us, was the last thing we needed.

As soon as I told Lucy I'd been offered the place, she asked me not to take it. It would be uprooting us, taking us up north away from friends and family. *I won't know anyone,* Lucy said. *I won't have that support.* She begged me. She cried. But I was so fixated on my job, was caught up in all of that, I wouldn't listen to her. *We're going,* I told her. *It's my career.*

Lucy was right. Not for the last time, she foresaw exactly what was going to happen. I did the training and the dark thoughts about Iraq got worse. I continued to be short and sharp with her. The situation at home deteriorated. I couldn't give her the help she needed with Bailey because of where my head was at; she couldn't turn to her parents or her friends for help and ended up being completely isolated.

We reached breaking point. Lucy turned to me one day and said, 'I can't do this any more.'

I snapped back at her, 'Well go, then.' And she did. Back down south, taking Bailey with her.

It wasn't just my relationship that reached crisis point. I got to a point as well with the instructing where I couldn't carry on. Part of that was because of Iraq, yes, but my headspace with that and with what was happening with Lucy, it was all over the place. I needed to get out of there. For the first time since I'd joined the army, I found myself questioning whether I'd made the right decision. I'd joined up when I was just sixteen years and nine months old – I'd never spent any real time out on Civvy Street. I had this growing desire to see what that sort of life would be like. I saw stepping out as a chance to get my shit back together. Maybe I would go out on Civvy and really enjoy it. Or maybe I'd get out there, realise that the army was the thing for me and come back in again. That's how I saw it, a sort of gap-year, time-out type of thing. But I had to do something, I came to realise. My head was in such a state with everything, that I needed to do something different.

I was meant to teach at Catterick for two years. But I ended up barely doing half of that before I told them my plans and took the plunge in October 2005 into the real world.

CHAPTER TWELVE

CIVVY STREET

THE INFANTRY FOOTBALL CLUB chairman was a gentleman called Colonel Richard Kemp. He is a great soldier – an absolute tactician, inspiration and one of the most intelligent officers that I have got to know. Before I went to Iraq, we'd had this Infantry dinner in London where I sat next to him. I told him where I was going and he said, 'Good lad. Make sure you fucking close and destroy the enemy.' When I got back from Iraq, I'd bumped into him again at an Infantry six-a-sides at Pirbright, which he was watching. 'What the fuck was that tour about?' he said. 'That was fucking madness.'

When I signed off from the army in Catterick, it was Richard Kemp who I reached out to. I explained what I was going to do and said to him, *If you hear of anything on the grapevine, then please do let me know.* A couple of weeks later, I got a call back from him. There was a very wealthy businessman, he said, who was looking for someone to look after him and his family, to chauffeur him around and be a sort of right-hand man for him. Was I interested?

The businessman in question was Lloyd Dorfman (now Sir Lloyd Dorfman CBE). In 1976, he'd set up a shop in currency exchange in Southampton Row in London. From here his business, Travelex, began to grow. After moving into Europe, the company had grown to the point that by the end of the 1980s, he was opening branches in countries from America to Australia. In 2001, Travelex became the world's largest non-bank foreign-exchange business and continued to expand into Asia in the following years.

So when I travelled down from Catterick to meet him, I was somewhat nervous to say the least. My first ever job interview and it was with one of the most successful businessmen in the country! I got to the interview in Kingsway half an hour early, which was pretty standard for me as I hate being late. I remember going into the Eat café next door to where we were meeting and sitting there for 20 minutes, feeling somewhat apprehensive. But when I finally went in and was ushered up to the boardroom to meet him, he couldn't have been nicer. The interview wasn't like a traditional interview at all, instead he asked me about my military career, something that he has a huge interest in.

We talked about what the job would entail. Lloyd explained that I would be doing a lot of driving round and would hear a lot of conversations as he was on the phone doing business. A lot of the stuff I'd hear was confidential, Lloyd said, and he needed a driver that he could trust absolutely. Whoever does this role, Lloyd continued, will need to keep that information to themselves and it wasn't to be talked about beyond the car or his home. Then he asked me whether I liked dogs. That seemed a slightly odd question, but I said that, yes, we'd had two Labradors growing up. Lloyd explained that he had two golden retrievers and that when he and his wife, Sarah, were away, they'd need taking out. 'That would be more than fine by me,' I said.

The conversation lasted 20 minutes. Shook his hand. Left the building. Then on the train on the way back, I got a call from Richard Kemp. 'Lloyd really likes you,' he said. Sure enough, I then got a call from Lloyd offering me the job. I finished up at Catterick and moved back south. Lucy had moved back in with her mum and dad, so I had our house to myself, which was a bit odd. It just felt a bit empty without Lucy and Bailey there. Plus, it wasn't very practical – Lloyd lived near Hampstead Heath, so I had to drive from Hampshire there and back each day. I got a flat with my mate Alfie in Borehamwood, which was about 15 minutes away which made a lot more sense.

It was a demanding job. Lloyd worked long hours, which meant that I worked long hours as well. But it was one hell of a learning curve for me. I'd listen to his conversations in the back of the car and it was the most remarkable insight into how one of our top business minds worked. The detail he'd go into was extraordinary. Nothing was overlooked, nothing left to chance. He was meticulous in his approach, which was probably why he was so successful. Hearing him speak and conduct his business was really inspiring. I knew one style of leadership from joining the army. But here was another, quite literally a different way of doing business.

At the same time, he was an incredibly generous guy as well. Over the years he has done a lot for the Jewish community, the Prince's Trust, our regimental charity, Great Ormond Street Hospital – there is even the Dorfman Surgery Centre there, named after his family. That generosity spread across his family. His wife, Sarah, couldn't have been kinder to me. They'd be going out and she would be getting my dinner sorted, so I wouldn't go out on an empty stomach.

Their kindness couldn't have been better timed. Because being there, in that flat at Borehamwood, was hard. I didn't have Lucy, I didn't have Bailey, I didn't have my family, I didn't have my mates in the regiment to chat with. Lloyd is a fantastic guy, but I was working for him, it wouldn't have been appropriate to discuss how I was feeling or what I was going through.

Most of all, I was lonely. I felt extremely isolated. In that flat, I had a lot of time to think. Overthink, in fact. I would dwell and brood on stuff, get myself into a state going over what I'd been through. It felt as though I'd lost everything that I'd loved. Lucy wasn't there to talk to, we'd just communicate by text over the arrangements of when I could see Bailey. The contrast between that and the time we used to spend together couldn't have been starker.

*

Lloyd had a big car. A Mercedes S-500, an absolute beast of a vehicle. I had been used to driving Warriors, so thought driving the S-500 was going to be a gift. But the gateway to Lloyd's house was quite narrow and I remember one time trying to get through and scraping the whole thing up on the side. I was so apologetic, said I would pay for the damage from my own money, but he wouldn't hear of it. *Just get it sorted and don't worry about it*, he told me.

Another time, I was delivering a document for him in the centre of town when I hit a cyclist. It was nine o'clock in the morning on the Strand and, as you can imagine, there were cars everywhere. I was waiting at a red light, but when it turned green and I went to move, this cyclist appeared out of nowhere. I slammed on the brakes but couldn't stop in time and he went smack into the side and on to the bonnet. Basically, he'd jumped the lights and I hadn't seen him. I got out and there was this volley of horns from behind because the traffic lights were on green and everyone wanted to get to work. We had a bit of an exchange, him going crazy at me, me telling him it was his fault. I was angry and from nowhere could feel myself reaching boiling point. I told him to move his fucking bike, but he got his phone out and started taking pictures. 'Look,' I said, 'I'm going to park up round the corner and we can discuss it there, because there's all these people going berserk behind me.' I got back in and drove around until I could find a space, which wasn't the easiest thing to do in central

London. By this point I was raging, the red mist was down. I ran back to where the accident took place, but when I got there the cyclist had gone. It was probably just as well, because I was out of control by this point.

I told Lloyd what happened, but thought no more about it. But the next thing I knew, I received a letter telling me that I was being charged with a hit-and-run. That seemed crazy, but it turned out the cyclist had taken a photo of the number plate and gone straight to the police. Even though it was his fault and I'd returned to sort it out, I was charged and taken to court.

Lloyd was typically calm about the whole thing, said he would get me a lawyer and sort it. But even with that support, it was a scary experience, going up in front of the three magistrates. It was the first time I'd ever been summoned to court and I was anxious in the run-up and nervous when I got there. I was extremely worried about the outcome and what the repercussions might be.

One of the judges wanted to let me off completely – *Look at his military record*, she said. *He's been to Iraq, awarded the Military Cross.* But the others disagreed – there was a benchmark set for cases of this kind and the evidence was against me. There was CCTV footage of me leaving the scene, but none showing the incident or proving that the cyclist was at fault. It seemed really unfair, but I had to plead guilty because of that. Potentially the consequences were harsh – a loss of my driving licence and a community-service sentence. In the end, they put nine points on my licence and fined me £500. The female magistrate was insistent until the end. *This is a mistake*, she told the other two. *He's never been in trouble before and we shouldn't punish him now.* But they were insistent that rules were rules and so I got fined.

Working for Lloyd wasn't the only change. Being apart from Lucy and Bailey also took more than a bit of getting used to. To be honest, it was killing me. Lucy was my rock and it felt weird not having her around, being in Borehamwood pretty much by myself. I'd already missed so much of Bailey growing up and it hurt to be missing even more. We agreed that I'd have Bailey to look after every other weekend and I always looked forward to those days. There was a leisure centre near the flat, so I'd take him swimming most weekends. We'd watch cartoons, go to the shops, do all sorts of stuff. The hardest part, sometimes, was going to pick him up. He and Lucy had such a special bond they'd built up that he didn't want to leave her. It wasn't that he didn't want to be with me, but to be away from his mum wasn't easy. The most obvious solution to that was to get back together, but when I broached that subject with Lucy she wouldn't even countenance it. So I'd see her picking up Bailey and dropping him back and that was it.

Over the months, though, things began to thaw a little. When I did the pick-ups or drop-offs, we'd have a little bit of a conversation. Just asking each other how we were.

Then after a while she started inviting me in for a drink. I was very respectful of her space. I never asked her about her personal life or anything like that. My thinking at this point was that if it was meant to be, it was meant to be, so I wasn't going to push it. That wasn't easy, because there were clearly still feelings there and I was still really attracted to her. And then there was Bailey as well. I didn't want the family to separate. But I knew that I needed the space to sort myself out before we could even think of getting back together. And it was the same, too, for Lucy.

The conversations at the pick-ups started to get a bit longer. We were talking more and then, one time, I suggested that we should go and have something to eat. 'No pressure,' I said, 'just to see what happens.' So that's what we did. We talked about my work with Lloyd, we talked about us, we talked about the army. By this point, in February 2007, I was starting to think about going back in, but I wanted to know what Lucy thought.

'If that is going to make you happy,' she said. 'If that is what you want to do, then you should do it.'

It was, I was increasingly realising, what I wanted to do. Every time I found myself chatting to mates, lads who were still serving, I had this pang. I would listen to them and realise that I missed the buzz of being on operations.

'What about us?' I asked. 'Where do you see ourselves going? I am not going to force anything, but there is clearly something here and it would be a shame to throw it all away.' I told her that I had learned from some of the mistakes that I had made and that I wouldn't make those mistakes again. 'I have been selfish,' I told her. 'Some of the decision-making has been selfish, I know that now and it won't happen again.'

I meant that. The time out, the time away from Lucy had really helped me to see that. Working for Lloyd, there was a lot of waiting around and that gave me plenty of time to think. I did a lot of analysing of stuff, working out where I had gone wrong and what it was I could do to make amends. There's no doubt, too, that being away from the army had helped me with the bad memories from Iraq. Those middle-of-the night sessions, those deep daydreams, those dropped right back. I still caught myself thinking about it from time to time, but nowhere near as often. They were more on the backburner now than at the front of my mind. And that really helped with the headspace, took the pressure off. My patience started to come back. I was less angry, less short-fused, more myself.

I said to Lucy not to make any decisions there and then, but to go away and have a think about things. So she did and to my delight she came back and told me that she wanted to give things another go. She thought that going back to Paderborn in Germany would work as a fresh start for both of us. I'd be back in the regiment and she'd be back among friends and people that she knew.

All that was left for me to do was to tell Lloyd. That was really hard. I'd grown fond of him and his family and really appreciated what they'd done for me. We had this routine where we used to train together most mornings. He had an indoor swimming pool at his house in Hampstead and a load of gym stuff including boxing gloves and pads. He'd just bought a yacht and I remember telling him that I should teach him some life-saving drills for that. So this particular morning, that was what we had been working on, while I was trying to pluck up the courage to tell him. We were both in the pool coming to the end of the session when I told him I had something to tell him. He knew immediately. 'Are you going back in?' he asked. And I said, yes, I was.

He was gutted. Gutted, but he respected my decision 100 per cent. I wasn't leaving him to work for someone else, but to go back into the army. It was a pretty emotional moment – I'd worked for him for a year and a bit, but had got to know him so well. There is a bond there between us and that is still there. Many years on, he is still there, looking out for me. I remember parking his car for the last time, handing my key fob back and then heading out of his big black wooden electric gates, and watching them slide shut behind me.

My time with Lloyd was a crucial chapter in my life. In terms of my headspace, in terms of my career, in terms of my marriage, it really helped to answer a lot of questions.

It was something I had to do and meant that I returned to the army refreshed, rejuvenated and ready to start again. That was better for everyone all round, but came with a sting in the tail that I wasn't to discover for years. My actions to save my career were the ones that, ironically, would turn out to end it.

CHAPTER THIRTEEN

BACK TO IRAQ

I RETURNED TO IRAQ for my second tour in 2008–9. The atmospherics compared to my first tour of Iraq could not have been starker. That tour had been seriously kinetic – action-packed and peppered with incidents. This tour, apart from a couple of particular moments, was painfully slow and drawn out. The only thing that stayed the same was how much I missed my family.

Back in 2004, the supposed peacekeeping tour had turned into one about trying to retain control of a province that didn't want the British there. The aftermath of the war was still much in evidence. Five years on, our presence was less about building bridges and more about packing and getting ready to go home. The withdrawal of British troops from the country had already been announced, so we were there to help in the dismantling of that set-up and to lay the groundwork for the subsequent handover to the Iraqi forces. We were the last main operational tour before the extraction.

The consequence of this was that I saw a lot less of Iraq this time round. Camp Abu Naji, I think, had already gone by this point and we found ourselves based instead at the somewhat more secure location of Shaibah Logistics Base.

There were no regular patrols into Basra as we had done in Al-Amarah. We didn't want or need to have a show of force, or create a situation where we were stirring up tension with our presence. The only time we went out, really, was when UK Special Forces were involved and they needed a cordon created. Instead we were on a constant QRF for six months – a quick-reaction force on notice to move, without ever actually receiving any notice to move. A bit like being a substitute for a football game, without ever actually getting called on to the pitch.

That brought its own challenges, not least in terms of motivation. It's when troops are bored that they do their own thing and bad things start to happen and mistakes begin to get made. But at the same time, if you give the troops tasks to keep them busy but which are essentially needless, that fucks them off as well. That was a difficult balancing act to get right. I was a platoon sergeant by this point, so I had a lot more responsibility than the first tour and this balancing act of maintaining morale landed right on my desk. We put on a lot of lessons – weapons handling, tactics and map reading. We did a lot of gym sessions too. But it wasn't easy.

On that first tour, you didn't have time to think. This time we had too much of it. And I think that was most difficult for the younger soldiers, who hadn't been out on operations before. I'd been there myself when I first joined. Excited about going to experience action and then discovering there wasn't really any. So they'd start getting bored and doing silly shit like skipping lessons to go and eat in the American sector.

The camp, compared to Abu Naji, was huge. It was a far slicker operation, too: conditions were a lot better, proper tents with air con and showers, rather than those container units we'd slept in the first time round. The whole set-up was more permanent and professional. The American sector, which was right on the other side of the camp, had amazing facilities. There was a Pizza Hut, a Burger King, a Subway, all sorts. There were a number of occasions where we'd be trying to do a lesson and there'd be people missing. The sergeant major would be right on my case – *Where are your fucking men, Woody?* And I'd be thinking, Oh they've fucked off to Pizza Hut, haven't they? And then we'd be on a mission to find them, bring them back and stick them on sangar duty.

Right back on that first tour in Kosovo, I'd been struck by the contrast between the resources of the British and American troops. Nearly a decade on, none of that had changed: they had better gear, better equipment, better food.

That difference wasn't just clear in the restaurants that the Americans had to offer on camp, but right down to the rations we were given to eat. One of the more interesting tasks on that second tour was when we got to go out to what was called Leaf Island. This was an island on the

River Tigris, from which boat patrols were sent out. The various platoons took turns to occupy the compound: you'd go out and spend a fortnight there and keep it secure, then it would be someone else's turn to do the same.

The food on tour was divided up into various menus – menu A, B, C, D, whatever. On one menu you'd get burger and beans for breakfast, then tomato pasta and treacle pudding for dinner. The next menu you'd have corned-beef hash, sausage and beans, omelette and so forth. Back at camp, the menus would get rotated round, but on Leaf Island that didn't happen. We were there for the fortnight and we'd be given the same rations every day. If you got menu C on day one, then it was going to be menu C for the rest of the stay.

Shortly after we arrived at Leaf Island for our stint, we were joined by a SEAL team from the US Special Forces. They had their own separate mission that they were down to do and we didn't get involved in that. But they were embedded with us in terms of where they were staying. We set up cot beds for them, where they'd rest up in between going out in the RIBs (a type of navy boat). For the younger lads in particular, that was a really useful and interesting experience – the SEAL team would come back in the morning and we'd sit around and talk about what it was like to be a special forces operator.

But while the SEAL team couldn't have been friendlier, they were less than happy with what we offered them to eat.

'Fucking hell,' the team commander said to me on the first day. 'What is this shit? These rations are stinking.'

'Mate,' I said, laughing, 'this is what we have got to eat for the next two weeks.'

'No way,' he said. 'They make you eat this shit?'

'Every day.'

'We've got to do something about that,' the SEAL team officer said. 'I've got to make some calls, get you some MREs.' MRE is the name for American rations – meals ready to eat.

'That would be great,' I said, thinking that would be an end to it.

The SEAL team were there for a week. When they left, the SEAL team officer said to me, 'When I get back to base, I'm going to make sure someone comes and drops you some MREs.'

Then three days later, I heard a noise in the distance. It sounded like a helicopter, though that couldn't have been right. We weren't due an underslung for a couple more days, hadn't secured the helipad in preparation or anything like that. *Helicopter inbound*, one of the sangars radioed in. What the fuck? I thought, scrambling to get things ready as it got closer.

Whup-whup-whup. As the dot in the distance got closer, I could see it was a Black Hawk. It flew in low and rather than an underslung, the guys in the back pushed out a couple of crates, which landed with a thump on the ground.

The door gunner hung out the door, gave me this big shit-eating grin and the thumbs up. Then it pulled up and he was away.

We rushed over to crack these crates open and they were full of MREs, ten-man ration packs. Cake, custard, biltong, peanut butter ... all kinds of stuff. It was quality, we had the best dinner ever that night. When we got back to the camp in Shaibah, I made a point of going over to the American sector to find him. I tracked him down and said thanks – *What you did was top drawer*, I told him, *and was really appreciated*.

He batted my thanks away. 'Nah, it's what allies do, you looked after us and made us welcome. The least we could do was to give you something to eat apart from that shit.'

If that was the lighter moment on the tour, the darker time was the death of one of our fellow soldiers, Ryan Wrathall (Socks). It had been fairly early on in the tour and the day had started out like any other. It was an early misty morning, one with the bite of a chill in the air and my platoon were getting ready to line our vehicles up. As platoon sergeant, I was going to inspect my men and the vehicles, that all the correct equipment and kit was in place. There were two cookhouses we used at the camp, one at the north, the other at the south, and on this particular morning, I'd had breakfast in the northern one. I finished that and then headed back to my tented accommodation to collect the rest of my kit.

As I leant over the wall by my bed to grab my body armour and webbing, I heard what sounded like a machine gun. It didn't sound right – dull and muffled – but I was instantly on alert. In camp we were unloaded, so no one should have had a loaded weapon with them, never mind it being made ready. I knew immediately that something serious must have happened.

I ran out. And as I did so, I heard someone shouting, *He's killed himself, he's killed himself!* from the tent next door to mine. I ran in to where the shouts were coming from. The first person I saw was Corporal Canes. He had his hands on his head. I asked him what had happened and he told me Wrathall had killed himself. I entered the tent and couldn't believe what I saw. There was a soldier, dead on the floor, and the stench of burning flesh. Crouched by him was his platoon sergeant, Dan Davey. He was shouting at Wrathall, 'Why have you done this?'

'What the fuck's happened?' I said, but looking at the body on the floor, the answer was fairly clear. The soldier, Private Ryan Wrathall, had loaded his LMG, put it in his mouth and fired. It was a horrific scene. I remember a medic rushing in, seeing the body on the floor and fainting. Dan, I think it was, handed me the LMG and I took it out to unload it. Wrathall had disconnected the belt from the LMG and put about five rounds into the feed tray. A full belt would carry 100 rounds, if that went off, you could end up with a runaway gun and all kinds of carnage. Socks knew that and knew what he wanted to do, so he'd loaded up the weapon accordingly.

The RMP appeared so I handed the weapon over to them. They looked at me and said, 'You'd better go and wash your hands.' I looked down and realised they were covered in blood. I went off to the toilets and tried to scrub myself clean.

Socks as Ryan was known, wasn't in my platoon, so I didn't know him well. But he'd been part of my company and living in the next tent to mine, so I knew who he was. It was a shocking incident and just desperately sad. I believe that he'd lost his dad earlier in the year. He'd been incredibly close to his father. Later it was discovered that he'd taken a large dose of morphine that morning, before fatally shooting himself.

The incident shook everyone up. Patrols were cancelled. The padre was brought in and he spoke to the soldiers, tried to make sense of it all. For me, it was something I wished that I hadn't experienced. Another image from Iraq that was set to haunt me, like the deaths and dead bodies from before. Those memories I'd had from before, they started to surface back up again.

It was to be almost another three years before I finally confronted these demons and received some professional help with my PTSD. By this point, the situation in the army had changed in terms of how they dealt with it. PTSD was increasingly becoming an issue and the army had to respond. There was a set-up called TRiM processing – Trauma Risk Management – which was starting to be put in place. Someone would come in and discuss the tour with you. *Are there any incidents that stood out for you? Is there anything that happened that you find yourself replaying again and again in your mind?* The questioning was all carefully geared to try and help you to open up. You'd get a colour-coded grading on your answers – green, amber or red. If you came back red, then you were sent to see someone who was a specialist.

When I came back from Iraq that second time, I think that set-up was still in its infancy and I didn't have those discussions. I went to instruct on a Royal Marines Senior Command Course. That was quite intensive, with a lot of work, and I remember one evening staying up with a mate of mine, who was a Royal Marines instructor, working on this report through the night. He'd been through a number of incidents as well – various casevac procedures in Iraq and Afghanistan – and he started speaking about that.

I'm still not sure why I did it, whether it was because it was someone I knew, someone who'd been through something similar and I thought they'd understand, but I found myself talking about Danny Boy. It was the first time I'd spoken about it to anyone, really, but there was something about the atmosphere that it just felt right to do so. So I started to explain to him about the enemy dead and having to deal with loading up the Warriors with the bodies. I was aware as I was talking that my mate had gone quiet and was sat there listening. He let me speak and, to my surprise, I did so.

'Mate,' he said, when I'd finished. 'You need to go and talk to someone about this. That is an event that happened, what, six, seven, eight years ago? And you're speaking about it as though it was yesterday.'

Looking back, I was lucky with the timing. My mate had recently been on a TRiM training course, so he was pretty clued up on the subject. He knew what signs and symptoms to look out for and when he heard me speaking he was immediately aware of what he was witnessing and what I might be going through.

'The best thing you can do,' he said, 'is to go and try and get some direction on your headspace, go and have a couple of sessions and see what happens.'

'I'm not sure,' I said. I was still in the mindset that going to seek help was somehow a sign of weakness.

'Just do it, Woody,' my mate said. 'What's the worst that can happen? No one has got to know about it. You are a senior colour sergeant, it is fine. Just go and see what the crack is.'

I was still uncertain, but I agreed to go. The first guy I went to see was a lieutenant colonel. This was at

Lympstone, and I was petrified. It was one thing talking to a mate of mine about it, but this was chatting cold to someone I didn't even know. When I went up to his office to see him, I reached my hand up to knock on the door and paused. Just knock on the door, a voice in my head was saying. It's no good, I can't do this, said another. I put my hand down and walked away.

I was back down the corridor, walking away, when I stopped. Come on Woody, I said to myself. Get a grip. I stood there for a minute, debating with myself, then turned round and went back to the lieutenant colonel's office. Before I could talk myself out of it again, I knocked on the door straight off.

'Come in.'

I took a deep breath and opened the door.

The lieutenant colonel, I didn't know him, but he was brilliant. God knows what I must have looked like, but he was immediately calming, reassuring, asking me if I wanted a coffee. I wasn't really sure what I was expecting, but it was less formal than I thought it might be and that helped me relax. Like my mate in the Royal Marines, this guy had seen plenty of action, done a tour in Afghanistan with 40 Commando and as he talked a bit about that, I could feel myself relaxing a bit more, feeling that this was someone who had been there, might understand. As he continued to speak, he explained how he talked to a lot of people in my position. He was very discreet, didn't mention any of the other cases, but the way he spoke about it, he made it clear that I was far from alone in feeling this way. And while it might not have been talked about publicly, having such thoughts was a lot more common than I might have realised.

'Thank you for coming to see me,' he said. 'And well done. I know it's not easy coming over to see me. The fact that you've done so, I really appreciate it.'

'I just want to clear my headspace a bit,' I said.

We started to talk. To begin with, he didn't ask about Iraq at all. Instead, we talked about my background, growing up, about Lucy and the boys. We spoke about football as well. This isn't so bad, I thought. This guy knew what he was doing, getting me to relax before getting on to the serious stuff. I can't remember whether he prompted me to talk about Iraq or whether I just launched into it, but before I knew it I found myself telling him about everything. About Danny Boy, the bodies, hearing the last breath of a dying militia man. I talked about Johnson Beharry, about me getting injured, about Adam Llewellyn and the petrol bomb. I talked, too, about Ryan Wrathall committing suicide. I don't know how long I spoke for, but when I came up for air I could sense that it had been a while.

'It's okay to have these emotions,' the lieutenant colonel said. 'It's what makes you human. It doesn't matter what sort of character you are, what organisation you are in, when you go through the sort of stuff you have been through, it's going to latch on.'

We talked through each incident I'd brought up. How I felt at the time, what I felt afterwards, how I felt now. It wasn't a therapy session in the strictest sense – the lieutenant colonel didn't offer any opinions or solutions. He didn't judge me, I think that was the thing I really noticed. He allowed me to speak and he just listened. And once I got the sense he wasn't going to pass judgement on how I felt, that really helped me to relax and open up. Just being able to talk, I can't really explain in words how that felt. But what I remember is leaving that room feeling like the world had been lifted from my shoulders. It was only from how light I felt afterwards that I realised just how heavily these memories had been pressing down.

After I finished talking, we went through a questionnaire. It was an open-question sort of thing, to get a sense of where my thoughts were at. Was I depressed at all? No, I didn't think I was. Did I have anxiety or panic attacks? Again, no. Did I have problems with anger and patience? Here, I did pause. Yes, I admitted. I had had issues there. I told him a little about Lucy and also about my football. I can't remember who commented on it, but having always been a relatively clean player, I'd started to have a bit of a discipline problem: yellow cards and sendings-off, flashpoint stuff where I'd respond.

I only had the one session with the lieutenant colonel and it was only a couple of hours long, but really, they were probably two of the most important hours of my life. From there, he recommended that I should see someone and he set me up with a therapist to speak to. He wasn't someone military based, but he had done a lot of work with soldiers in my situation. So much so, that he came on to camp to do the sessions. In total, I think I did about ten hours with him in five two-hour sessions.

The therapist went into more detail than the lieutenant colonel had done. He really drilled down, went a lot deeper on a number of issues. He really concentrated on my feelings and emotions and tried to get to the bottom of those. Just like the lieutenant colonel, he told me that it was okay to feel like I was and repeated that I wasn't the only soldier to go through this. What he said that was different to what the lieutenant colonel had said was that he brought in my family.

'You've started on the right journey to look after you and your family,' he told me. 'As much as it might seem it, this isn't just about you. Yes, these events have had a huge effect on you, but they are also affecting people who love you and care about you.'

That made me stop and think. I'd been so focused on myself, that I hadn't really thought about how it affected Lucy and the boys. I'd tried to protect them by not talking about it, about trying to keep those feelings to myself. But as I talked to the therapist, I got to understand the effect that decision has had on them and on others.

Those sessions helped me get a better sense of what it was I'd been through. In the short term, that understanding made me a better leader.

About two years after our tour to Afghanistan, in August 2013 we were out in Canada doing some training. There were a couple of the lads there who were really going haywire, getting emotional and breaking down in tears. One guy was in such a state, he smashed a window through. Turned out they had been out on the beer, got talking about an incident that had happened to them in Afghan and completely lost it. I didn't mention to them what I'd been through, but because I'd had those experiences, because I'd seen this therapist, it meant that I got a sense of what they were going through. Before I'd had the therapy sessions, I'd have probably bollocked them royally for breaking that window. But now, to their surprise, I said not to worry about it. 'We can sort that out, but the important thing is to get you calmed down.'

'I can't change what's happened to you,' I said, 'but we can help in getting you better.'

And I put them in touch with people who could.

I still haven't enacted everything that the therapist told me. Even now, several years on, I still feel I'm on a learning curve in dealing with what I've been through. I'm making progress, one step at a time. The therapist said that I should try and talk to friends, and to Lucy, about what happened. But that's really hard. I've done a number of speaking events where I've talked about my time in Iraq and in a strange way I find it easier to talk to a packed room full of hundreds of people I don't know than to sit down and speak with the one person who knows me best.

With the speaking events, whether it is to schools or organisations, or businesses or whatever, I'm trying to make something positive about what I've been through. And talking about those events in public really helps. In early 2018, I agreed to speak at an event in my local village to raise money for charity. The fact that it had sold out in two hours and they had 115 people coming to hear me speak, that didn't bother me at all. The fact that Lucy was going to be there, that my dad was flying down from Edinburgh for it, that both of them were going to hear the whole story of what I'd been through from start to finish for the first time, that was terrifying. But it felt the right thing to do. I felt ready to do it. And so, finally, I did.

I'm so glad I did that. Not only had I not talked to Lucy about what happened, I hadn't even told her that I had been to see someone and have these sessions. 'Why didn't you tell me?' she asked when she found out about them. 'Because you have got your own issues to worry about,' I said. 'But your issues are my issues,' Lucy replied. 'That is what we do for each other.' Maybe, looking back, I should have tried to talk to her about it earlier. But now she does know about what I went through, I would say that we are the strongest that we have ever been. Proper solid. There is a bright future for us and the boys. And that's really exciting.

I'm not the finished article on dealing with what happened in Iraq, even now. In a way, I'm not sure that I will ever be. Part of the process in dealing with this sort of stuff, perhaps, is learning to understand that and learning to accept that. Looking back, I was just so young when all this happened. As my mate Danny said to me once, 'How could you go into a fucking trench like that when you could barely even tie your own shoelaces?' Only now, all these years later, am I old enough to finally start making sense of it all.

CHAPTER FOURTEEN

THE FINAL TOUR

THE THERAPY SESSIONS that I had didn't last for long. That was because I was due to return to Germany, so I packed up the car and drove me and the family back there. We re-bedded and reintegrated, but I'd be moving before I knew it. My battalion was already in Afghanistan and I was put on the BCR (battlefield casualty replacement) list. I was told I was going to take over as a CQMS (company quartermaster sergeant). Before long, the call came in for me to start what, it turned out, would be my final military tour.

This last tour was always going to be different for me, because by this point we had Charlie as well, so it was two sons I was leaving behind. Bailey was eight and Charlie was two. It never gets easier, saying goodbye. Never gets any easier. You have this real heavy sensation in your stomach because of the experience of previous tours. I knew how much I'd miss them and I knew, from that first Iraq tour in particular, how deadly a tour could be. Then, just before I went, Tom Lake was taking part in a patrol to reassure the local population in the Jamal Kowi area of the Nahr-e Saraj district of central Helmand when he was caught in an explosion. He was airlifted to the field hospital in Camp Bastion, where he was declared killed in action. The blast also caused a further five casualties with ball-bearing injuries, with soldiers being flown back to the UK for surgery. Corporal Jones had really bad damage to his calf which meant he couldn't go back. We knew all that as we were prepping, getting all the intel about the atmospherics, which made it even harder to say goodbye to the family.

Lucy had always understood what my job entailed. We never discussed the what-ifs before going on tour because it is a hard conversation to have and you want to be thinking positive thoughts. You write a will out before you go away so everything is in place, insurance and that sort of thing. But to sit down and discuss that I could potentially be killed in action, that was too much to talk about, especially as I was now a father with two kids growing up. It was hard enough that Bailey was now at an age where he got what was going on. It is an emotional morning, packing your bags, saying goodbye to your loved ones. Any soldier will tell you that.

The role that I had been assigned was in Nahr-e Saraj Helmand, at one of the company checkpoints. The company were given an area of operations to hold as part of the 5 RIFLES battle group. We were in a checkpoint called CP Jeker; it was a central headquarters where the OC, the CSM and CQMS were. I was there as the CQMS, dealing with the whole logistical side of weapons – ammunition, water, rations, batteries and so forth – supplying and resupplying the checkpoints that were forward of us.

Jeker wasn't a big compound. I reckon there was probably 25 to 30 people staying there, max, a far smaller set-up than the camps I'd been to in Iraq. The checkpoint was based around a traditional Afghan compound, built out of mud walls, but which we'd then adapted with hessian and sangars. There were three or four sentry posts, all of which were manned 24/7, but thankfully they were never needed while I was there. The other checkpoints weren't far away, a couple of miles, perhaps, and we could hear them having scraps and dust-ups in the distance.

My role on this tour was a support role rather than a fighting-soldier's role, but I would still leave the security of the compound and go out, either in one of the Husky vehicles or on my quad bike with a trailer to do the resupplies. That's nerve-wracking, with the threat of IEDs, and you were really relying on the route to be cleared before you went through. You never knew what might happen in an environment like Afghan. In the back of your mind, you always had that thought: Is my luck about to run out?

I had not been a CQMS before, so I was really getting thrown in the deep end to take on an operational account. Anyone will tell you, taking over a CQMS role is a demanding process, but then to go operational and do it and hand over in a war zone it was doubly hard. Just taking over, you had to go to all of the checkpoints and go through all the weapon accountability, the optic accountability, the ammunition accountability – all when people and kit were out on patrol. In total, the handover with the CQMS took over a week to do.

Being CQMS is the kind of role that everyone tries to avoid, as it means you are not soldiering any more. You are not a decision-maker on the front line. It is a natural progression for any infantry soldier that you go in and take over as a CQMS. It normally lasts for two years and once you have got your tick in the box for running an account and the promotion board sits, you're in with a shout to become CSM.

It was an odd feeling, being out and not being at the sharp end. Talk to any commander and nine times out of ten they'll tell you they'd rather be out there themselves. But I knew that the guys had been on the ground a lot longer than me. By the time I arrived, they'd been there for three months already, so understood the battle picture and mission command, absolutely knew the atmospherics. In that situation, you just have to take yourself out of it and trust them. You re-role. I'd be in a patrol and I would go out with the platoons, visit the checkpoints. I was taken out by corporals and I just acted as a private soldier. You totally respect the commanders because they are very good at what they do.

Hey, Colour, they'd shout at me. *We are going on patrol, do you want to come out with us?* I'd say yes, because I wanted to get out of the compound. I'd be there as a sixth man, taken through the orders process as though I was a normal soldier. I would sit in as a bod and go out on the ground, just to see what they did day-to-day. Luckily on those patrols, nothing went wrong, no kinetic engagement or any explosions going off.

In that sense, the back end of that tour was relatively quiet. But my time in Afghanistan had its own demands with the accounts. They were different pressures to what I had been used to as a commander growing up and being in situations, and they brought with them challenges of their own. Every infantry soldier has that moment when they go in from the sharp end of the bayonet to the logistics side. You know that is the natural progression. I knew I had to do it and I was prepared to do so.

When I went out to Afghanistan, it was cold initially. It was the wet season and pissing down with rain. But the month or so before we came home, it was getting really hot, 'redders' as we'd say. But it was a different type of heat to Iraq. That was a dry, blistering heat, this was a bit more humid. Where we were was farmland really. A lot of crops, a lot of irrigation ditches. In the winter the fields were cut and levelled, but by the time we were leaving it was a sea of green, the crops growing with the poppies coming up. There was opium everywhere. The place was riddled. It had its own sweet sort of stench you could smell when you were out or when the wind blew.

There were other differences between my time in Iraq and Afghan, too. The technology had changed, as had the kit. I remember being in Iraq in 2004 and my fighting kit was a mixture of desert and DPM (Disruptive Pattern Material) because we did not have desert webbing and day-sacks. The DPM was like the conventional stuff, the green camouflage. Handy in the desert! Back then, we'd have tiny little body armour plates on our chest, now we were full Kevlar all the way across the front and back. The weapons systems had evolved, too. The Sharpshooter weapons had been brought in. Looking back, we were behind the times in 2004 with our kit and equipment.

Communication back home didn't really change. You had better computers, which was great if they didn't break. But they very often did and never really got fixed, so you were very lucky if you got on the Internet. So it was back to having your card and your sat phone and 20 minutes a week to talk back home. That was no different to how it was when I was in Kosovo. Those conversations were the same as ever. You can't discuss what you are doing, so it's all, *Is everything okay? Good. What have you been up to? Fine. I'm glad everything is well. I will speak to you in three days' time. Or two days' time.* Those small, sharp conversations which I'd got into the rhythm of by now.

The terrain in Afghanistan was completely different. The Iraq tour was about city fighting, which is really hard. It is rooftop after rooftop after rooftop we were getting engaged from, and alleyways. Afghanistan, or where I was anyway, didn't have those demands of urban fighting. We were down in the valleys, there were mountains all around but where we were wasn't that hilly. But what there was, which Iraq didn't have so much, was IEDs. The place was riddled with them. In Iraq, there were a few remote IEDs; in Afghanistan, they were everywhere.

Travelling to another compound was a slow process. If I was on my quad bike, I would have a section which would be doing a foot patrol. They would stake the route, make sure it was secure and patrol alongside me. The journey to the next checkpoint might only be about a mile and a half to two miles max, but it would take us probably 55 minutes to get there. You needed eyes on constantly, with so many IEDs about, you had to be careful. But compared to the kinetic activity of Iraq, it was slow.

The pace might have been slow, but you could never relax. The threat was always there. You just didn't know what to expect in Afghanistan, so you were on your toes all the time. The minute you switch off, that's when the shit goes noisy, so you make sure you are alert. You have always got the butterflies, you have always got the adrenaline.

Back at the camp, we'd try to kick back in different ways. There was a gym within the compound, which I'd use. I say gym, it was essentially a few improvised weights! We'd watch DVDs and play board games. We were lucky that we'd get a lot of stuff sent out to us. Not just from friends and family, but from members of the public. We never asked for support in that way – we were there because we'd chosen to be in the army – but we were always incredibly grateful for people's generosity. Sometimes it would be food: noodles, biscuits and other items that made a change from the regular food we were eating. At other times it would be hand wipes, toothpaste, toothbrushes, flip-flops or board games. So we had Monopoly, Guess Who? and Risk, which we'd play to pass the time. We built up a good library of DVDs too, usually comedies or action.

There was a TV in the canteen with satellite. There was a BFBS (British Forces Broadcasting Service) box with four channels we could watch. Most mornings, a lot of us would go in and watch Susanna Reid, who was on *BBC Breakfast* at the time. She is a very good-looking lady and it was a little morale boost for us. We'd go in there, watch the news and get our daily fix of Susanna Reid before cracking on and going out on patrol.

What I didn't know, when I was watching those programmes, was that it wasn't going to be too long before I ended up going on breakfast television and being interviewed myself. Because while I might have finally begun to deal emotionally with what happened to me in Iraq, the legal implications that had been rumbling away in the background were about to become headline news and dominate my life in a way that I could never have anticipated.

CHAPTER FIFTEEN

AL-SWEADY

THE FIRST TIME I heard about the Al-Sweady Inquiry was when I was on the All Arms Commando Course in December 2009 to earn my green beret down at Lympstone. I had been chosen to instruct on that Royal Marines Senior Command Course, where I opened up to my mate about Danny Boy, and I felt I needed to have a bit of credibility with those I was going to instruct. Firstly, I was younger than the Royal Marines who were on their Senior Command Course. And secondly, I was external. I was in the army and I was going down to a naval environment, which is different to what I had been used to. There's always a bit of rivalry and banter between the army and bootnecks – they call us Pongos because they think the army never wash. So I wanted to do the commando course to make sure I didn't give them any more ammunition to come back at me with.

The course itself was tough. It was nine weeks in total, with a bottom field test after week five. You had to meet certain criteria to continue on. Weeks one to five were a proper thrashing on physical training, to get you to a point where you were ready to attempt the bottom field assault pass off. You have to do it in a certain time, otherwise you are gone and returned to your unit. Week nine was test week: you do the Tarzan assault course – that's the zip line high obstacle course; then onto the bottom field course, and you finish with a 30-foot wall climb. When you get to the top of that, your time stops. That's tough enough, but you're doing that with 21 pounds of kit on and your rifle slung. You do those, a 9-mile speed march, the endurance course – which is one of the hardest events – and finally the 30-miler. Then you have a ceremony the day after, when you get properly presented with your green beret in front of family and friends.

The course was both demanding and frustrating. It was frustrating because for me I was going back to basics – the course had to cater for all arms, so they had to start from the beginning. I was someone who'd done four operational tours, yet I was being taught how to clean my weapon and having to lay my kit out for inspection by a corporal, who I outranked. But I just had to deal with that side of things.

Other parts of the course were more challenging. The rope climb I found hard because I just did not have the technique. You should use your legs a lot more than your forearms but I was doing it the other way round. I'd get three-quarters to the top of the rope and my arms were burning out. I was so determined, though, that I would get up before anyone else was awake and go down to the gym where they had a PTI (physical training instructor) and I would do remedial rope climbs to try and sort my technique out. It was real graft.

For the final exercise, the weather was horrendous. It was winter and throughout the course it was wet and cold. Because I had a lot of experience of being a front-line soldier, I just got on with it. It was what it was. That was what we did. But there were people on that course with all sorts of cap badges and they could not do it. They were not mentally ready and fit enough to cope with the weather. For the first few days it did not stop raining and there were lots of people VW-ing (voluntarily withdrawing) from the course. I think about 40 people started the course and only about 20 passed.

The 30-miler at the end was tough. It took you across Dartmoor, over really demanding terrain and completely exposed to the weather. You finish by crossing a bridge – one of those famous landmarks in military circles. Get over that in the time limit – eight hours – and you have earned your green beret. That's tight. There's an instructor at each checkpoint who lets you know how you are doing and whether you need to speed up or slow down. If you're too far behind, then you are told you are now unsafe to carry on and are not going to make it. For me, though, the 30-miler wasn't an issue. Once I'd done the ropes I knew I was going to pass, since nothing else was really a massive issue because of what I had done previously and my experiences as a front-line soldier with my regiment.

The ceremony at the end of the course is cool. You get to invite your friends and family down and they do the presentation in the theatre. You get your green beret presented to you by the commandant of the Commando Training Centre, and usually commanding officers from other regiments come down as well to say congratulations. It's a great event, they even show your friends and family a video of what you have to go through on the course. Lucy came down to watch the presentation, as did a couple of friends.

But as satisfying as getting the green beret was, and as pleasing as the congratulations at the ceremony were, my mind wasn't totally on it. I kept going back to a phone call I'd got from Lucy during the course, with news about the inquiry.

In the years after the Battle of Danny Boy, there had been an increasing clamour for some sort of inquiry into the events that had taken place that day, both in terms of the actions on the battlefield and also what had happened on our return to Camp Abu Naji.

In the immediate aftermath of the battle, Camp Abu Naji had been visited by the ICRC (International Committee of the Red Cross). Allegations had been made by the Iraqi prisoners and the ICRC had asked the British to investigate. They did, in the form of the RMP, who had then turned up to interview me and the other soldiers involved – first at Abu Naji and then later when I was back in Brecon on that training course.

Those initial investigations produced little to back up the allegations. But the claims continued and were picked up by human rights lawyers, in particular Phil Shiner, who ran a firm called Public Interest Lawyers (PIL), and Martyn Day, of the firm Leigh Day. Phil Shiner had been involved in the case of Baha Mousa, an Iraqi who had died in British custody in September 2003. Mousa's autopsy showed that he received a number of injuries and in 2006 a number of soldiers were charged with assault and the inhumane treatment of detainees. One soldier pleaded guilty to inhumane treatment and was jailed for one year and expelled from the army. The other six had all charges of wrongdoing against them dropped, with the judge noting that 'none of these soldiers has been charged with any offence, simply because there is no evidence against them as a result of more or less obvious closing of ranks.' In 2008, the MoD paid out just under £3 million in compensation to Baha Mousa's family and nine other men who had also been arrested, due to what was described as 'substantive breaches' of the European Convention on Human Rights.

The case of Baha Mousa had absolutely nothing to do with what happened at Danny Boy. It had taken place at a different camp, in a different year and involved a different regiment. But what the judgement of that case did was to help change attitudes towards accusations against the British Army. Coupled with cases of torture and prisoner abuse involving American forces, such as Abu Ghraib in particular, the perception in the media grew that mistreatment by coalition forces was a regular occurrence. A section of the media, too, was increasingly critical of both the war and Britain's ongoing involvement; such stories of mistreament, then, only served to reinforce this narrative. The fact that the compensation offered in cases such as Baha Mousa's was so large only increased the number of accusations against the British Army still further.

On the back of all of this, the accusations about Danny Boy resurfaced. A group of six Iraqis – five involved in the battle and the uncle of Hamid al-Sweady, one of those killed – claimed that they had been ill-treated by British troops. Rather than being insurgent fighters, they said they were innocent civilians, farmworkers who had been caught up in the crossfire. Rather than the insurgents being killed on the battlefield, the men claimed they had been captured alive and then murdered back at the British base.

The MoD dismissed the allegations, saying 'we have found no credible evidence that those detained as a result of the attack on British troops and prolonged firefight at the Danny Boy checkpoint were mistreated.' Phil Shiner, however, disagreed. He claimed there was 'very credible evidence there was clear ill-treatment'. He said that 'these allegations are incredibly serious yet the Government has continuously delayed dealing with them since they were first made in 2004.' He wanted a public inquiry to look into the accusations.

Because of Shiner's involvement in the Baha Mousa case, he had a lot of credibility when it came to accusations about human rights violations. In February 2008, he published a dossier of allegations about Danny Boy. There were accusations of torture by British troops, the mutilation of bodies and the suggestion that up to 20 Iraqi captives may have been executed. Martyn Day claimed that 'the nature of a number of the injuries of the Iraqis would seem to us to be highly unusual in a battlefield.' He went on to suggest that Danny Boy might be 'one of the most atrocious episodes in British army history'. He said, 'the burning question for us as a nation is whether these 24 hours represented the British army at its best or the British army at its worst.'

Phil Shiner said that the British Army had either been involved in 'acts of immense bravery or acts of incredible brutality'. He said, 'we're not saying we know what happened; we're saying on the balance of probabilities we think our clients are telling the truth.' He went on to make comparisons with mistreatment by soldiers in previous conflicts: 'We do not want to be talked about in the same vein as the Japanese in the Second World War or the Americans at My Lai, but unless we stand up and say as a nation that this cannot happen in our name, this is where we seem to be headed.'

The claims by Phil Shiner and Martyn Day were swiftly followed by a *Panorama* documentary in which Shiner was interviewed. 'On Whose Orders? What Really Happened After the Battle of Danny Boy?' aired on Monday 25 February 2008. The programme said that it had spent a year talking to battlefield survivors, medical staff and former

Iraqi prisoners. In the programme, Shiner repeated his accusation that 'British soldiers may well have been responsible for the execution of up to 20 Iraqi civilians.' The *Panorama* programme said that 'we've seen no proof that anyone was killed at Abu Naji, let alone the 20 dead claimed by the lawyers for the Iraqis.' But it also concluded that in terms of the mistreatment of prisoners, 'the evidence we've heard is clearly worthy of investigation and fits the pattern from the Baha Mousa case.'

Despite the government continuing to deny any wrong doing on the past of the British soldiers, Greater Manchester Police were brought in to look at the original RMP investigation. Their findings were released in July 2009 and were heavily critical of the RMP investigation. They accused the RMP of failing to collect forensic evidence and ignoring key witnesses, among other criticisms. The following month, a judicial review began, along with a case at the High Court against the MoD by the six Iraqis. In October 2009, three High Court judges ruled against the MoD, accusing it of 'lamentable' behaviour and 'serious breaches' of duty over its investigation into Danny Boy. Given all of that criticism, the momentum behind having a public inquiry into Danny Boy became overwhelming. In November 2009, the defence secretary, Bob Ainsworth, announced that a public inquiry would be held. It would be called the Al-Sweady Inquiry, after one of the Iraqis who had been killed.

*

The call from Lucy came in the latter stages of the commando course. She told me there'd been a letter from the solicitors to say that there was going to be a public inquiry regarding the Battle of Danny Boy.

That was the first I'd heard of it. My immediate reaction was one of shock.

'Are you sure?' I asked Lucy. 'Is that letter definitely for me?'

'It's got your name and address on it.' She read the letter out again. 'There's going to be a public inquiry regarding Danny Boy.'

I rang up my regiment. I can't remember who I spoke to, but I called back to camp to find out what was going on. They confirmed what Lucy had said: there was going to be a public inquiry into the events surrounding Danny Boy. The allegations that were being made were extraordinary: that Iraqi prisoners had been mistreated, tortured and murdered. The inquiry meant these allegations were out in the open – out in the press; had gone public.

I was dumbfounded. Firstly, because of the nature of the allegations in comparison to the events that had taken place. But secondly, because I'd had no inkling that this inquiry was about to happen. I was away from my regiment doing the course, so I was a bit out of it in that sense. But I'd heard no rumours, nothing on the grapevine that this was about to be announced. So that all took me by surprise. I had to try and switch off from all that and crack on with the course I was on, and deal with it all when I got back. But that wasn't easy, believe me.

Once I'd finished the course, the letters really started to come in. I'd been assigned a solicitor by the MoD to represent me, and they started to explain what was going to be spoken about, what the allegations were saying and what sort of questions I was going to be asked when I got to the inquiry. I hadn't really considered what a public inquiry would consist of, but the thought of going up on the stand, being cross-examined over what I'd done – even though I hadn't done anything – that terrified me. That court case involving the cyclist in London had been stressful enough. But this was of a completely different magnitude.

When I got back from the commando course I went in to see the solicitors. I was due to go out to Afghanistan on tour, and was straight back into training for that, so I had to get stuff sorted before I went. The solicitors were based at No.#1, Kingsway. They explained what was being said and went through the accusations. I was told they'd looked at some of the evidence of the Iraqis and it wasn't very credible, which was a relief. But even so, they couldn't answer the questions I wanted answering: *Is everything going to be okay? Will I be called to give evidence?*

We went back and forth through the original statements I'd given. The first statement I'd given to the RMP was really terrible – in the sense that it hadn't been that detailed, because of in the questions they'd asked me. With the inquiry, they needed a more detailed account, so I answered question after question to pull my statement together.

I had endless questions to answer. *Did you see anyone, did you hear shots when you were in camp when the prisoners were taken back? Did you at any point hear a generator running and shots being fired? Did you see anyone on that position?* The questions got ever more bizarre: *Did you see someone taking someone's eyeball away from their sockets?* And all sorts of weird stuff. What the fuck is this? I thought. I'd given my statements before. Now I was being asked again, years later, to try and remember the events in minute detail – cross-checking my memory with the accusations made by the Iraqi prisoners.

That took months – them checking details, sending it over to make sure I was happy with it, me signing to say I was and then sending it back. The process seemed endless. I did the commando course in the winter of 2009. Then there was this endless questioning for the best part of 18 months. My statement was finally presented to the inquiry in February 2013, four years on. And then my appearance at the inquiry wasn't for another nine months. From my perspective, the process dragged on and on. It was only in 2013 that it finally got confirmed that I was going to be called to give evidence. Even then, I can't remember if I was told that my appearance would be in November of that year.

Not everyone who was questioned was summoned to give evidence. For some people, it was considered that their involvement did not warrant an appearance. But none of us knew that ahead of time – we made our statements, submitted them and waited to discover who was going to be called in. Not that we were comparing notes. We were told not to speak to people who were going through the same thing, to avoid any confliction. Though, to be honest, we never really did that anyway – we had separated off within the battalion, in different companies, and also none of us really wanted to talk about what we had gone through. We all wanted to forget about it. I wanted to deal with it how I wanted to deal with it, which was just to shut up shop and take it on the chin.

But even if I didn't want to talk about it, and the soldiers didn't want to talk about it, there were plenty of people who did. When I'd had that original phone call with Lucy, she'd been really concerned. I told her not to worry, that I would sort it out. But that turned out to be easier said than done.

CHAPTER SIXTEEN

ALLEGATIONS AND PREPARATIONS

IT WASN'T JUST Lucy who got in touch. When news of the inquiry got out, friends started messaging me, saying, 'We've just seen this on the news. What's going on?' They knew I'd been involved in Danny Boy and wanted to know what was happening. I found myself having to justify myself and what I'd done.

It was a difficult period for me, especially when I returned from the course. While I was in Lympstone, I had managed to park everything within my headspace. But once I was back, there was no escape. I couldn't really believe the coverage or the accusations that were being made. That the Iraqi prisoners were openly being called victims, without any evidence to back that claim up. Anyone who didn't know what had happened looked at those reports and thought, Fucking hell, they were unlawfully killed, they must be innocent civilians caught up in this, otherwise why would the media be calling them victims?

From my perspective, the decision to call an inquiry was all wrong. They had gone public without really understanding the factual evidence and the effect on those who the accusations were made against. It felt as though the media coverage hung us out to dry and the government, in my opinion, let them do that. They could have really stamped down and thought, Hang on a minute, do you know what damage it is going to cause if we release this without going through the proper checks? They should have done the factual research first and then launched it. Instead, they put my name and my regiment's name and the British Army's name right up in the public eye when it did not need to be. I still don't really understand the decision to go public so soon without gathering all of the information first, without speaking to me and everyone else involved.

We were British soldiers. We were sent to war to do what we'd been told by politicians, only to then come back and find ourselves fighting another battle to clear our names. At no point did anyone sit me down and go through everything that was going on. No one asked whether I'd need any support when it went public. Whether my family were okay. No one seemed to have considered whether their decision might put people at risk. It put me and my family's lives in danger because of who we were up against. My name was out there and you just didn't know what the response might be. I was hit unawares and left to ride this fucking mammoth wave and I tried to take each day as it came really.

The emotional impact was huge. I'd gone from being rewarded for my actions by Her Majesty the Queen to having the government undermine what I'd achieved by being happy to put all this out in the limelight and all over the media. Of course there has to be an understanding of human rights in how the troops behave. But there has to be a duty of care, too, to the soldiers involved. There was none of that for those of us dealing with what had happened out on the battlefield.

Ultimately, it was us who paid the price for the government's mishandling of the inquiry. They could have brought in an organisation like the Red Cross and said, 'Look, we will allow you to internally investigate this by all means but we are not going to go and make this a public inquiry because it can bring danger to the soldiers' lives.' After all, it wasn't hard for anyone to go and see who was alleged to be involved. Having a public inquiry was upsetting to those involved; it damaged families, damaged careers and fuelled PTSD.

Even now, this is why I feel hurt by the government. They could have flexed their muscles and said, 'We will look into this but it is going to be behind closed doors.' I lost trust and faith in the system. When I needed it most it failed me. And it hurt.

The reaction of some of the public was tough, too. It is hard to have put your life on the line and then to come back and hear things like 'Well, you probably should not have been there in the first place.' But I am not the decision-maker. I joined the military as a front-line soldier. I had been ordered to go out there and therefore I went and carried out the mission that had been put in front of us. That is the role of a British soldier. I follow a command and I go with it whole-heartedly. Because if you don't do that, once you start questioning the command structure, that is when it starts getting tricky and people's lives are put at risk.

Public opinion is swayed by what they read in the media. And there were some serious allegations out there. In 2005, three soldiers from the Royal Regiment of Fusiliers were jailed and dismissed from the army with disgrace for their treatment of prisoners on their watch. These incidents, though, were anything but the norm. Ninety-nine times out of a hundred, the standards and values of the British Army were adhered to. But when these sort of isolated inci-dents get into the press, then it's easy for people to read their paper and think, They're all like that. It wasn't helped when false allegations started getting out there, too. In 2004, the *Daily Mirror* printed pictures purporting to show abuse of Iraqi detainees by members of the Queen's Lancashire Regiment, which later turned out to be fake – leading to the departure of its editor, and an unreserved apology from the newspaper's board.

For those on the front line, such accusations did not do us any favours. At one end of the scale we've found that British soldiers have made a mistake and then at the other end of the scale we are getting this fake news being pub-lished, and the vast majority of us are stuck in the middle between the two. And though those *Daily Mirror* stories were revealed to be false, they added to the mood music at the time and caused us more pain than the press could possibly imagine. It is hard enough trying to be a front-line soldier without having all this stuff in the background.

Back when I was in Iraq on that first tour, these stories had an impact as we tried to build relations with the local population. That was why maybe the Americans were hit hard on a number of occasions, because of the video and picture evidence that these isolated individuals were being unlawful. And after Danny Boy, some of the Iraqis claimed that we'd taken the prisoners back and killed them in camp. The next day we were hit doubly hard. That is how it was – people making up lies to cause a stir and getting people to fight.

The truth was that we were trained, we were prepped. Before any tour, you do your pre-deployment training, which is about four and a half months long, and you go through all sorts of scenarios, all sorts of situations, in terms of how you should treat prisoners. You're told about the Geneva Conventions, you talk about the Rules of Engagement or the Guidance Card Alpha, which outlines what you can and cannot do. This is all spoken about. And you adhere to it.

Back home, people read the papers, watched TV and drew their own conclusions. One time, I had a situation where Bailey came home from school saying how he'd heard from the other kids that I'd unlawfully killed civilians. You know what kids are like, they will see things in the press or online or hear others talking and then all of a sudden there is speculation and schoolyard gossip, anything to get a rise out of someone else.

Bailey is quite an uncommunicative child and it can be hard getting him to say what is troubling him. He will open up to Lucy a lot more than he will with me. This particular evening, I remember going up to see him in his bedroom and he was quite upset.

'Hey,' I said. 'What happened, mate? What is going on?'

'Nothing,' he replied.

It took me a while to tease it out of him, but I could see he was upset, so I stuck it out until he told me.

'Kids at school,' he finally explained. 'They're going around saying that you killed innocent civilians.'

That stopped me in my tracks. 'Hey,' I said. 'That's just not true, okay? It's just speculation and it's nonsense. You mustn't believe what they tell you.'

I tried to explain how I'd been out to Iraq to do a job, that I had gone out there to serve my country. But it's difficult to explain all that and difficult for a kid to really understand what you'd been through. And for all my words, it was Bailey who was going to have to go back to school and face those comments. To be fair to the kids who'd spoken to Bailey, they later went back to him and apologised for what they'd said, which is a big thing for someone that age to do. But even so, it showed what was out there, what people thought. And it showed, too, that the accusations about my conduct didn't just affect me.

In the end, I think the incident wound me up more than him. I had to really grit my teeth, seeing him upset because of something I was supposed to have done. I wanted to rise above it all and say, 'Look, I was cleared of everything. It was completely all lies and speculation.' But it upset him, upset me and upset Lucy, too, to the point where I was all for going into the school and talking to his teachers about what had been said. I wanted to know where the kids had got their information from. Had they found that out themselves on the Internet, or were they repeating what their parents had told them? Lucy and I stayed up all night discussing it, trying to work out the best way to deal with it all.

Later, Lucy said to Bailey that he should have told them his dad got the Military Cross from the Queen for bravery. *How would he get awarded that if he'd been involved in something like that?* I don't really speak about the Military Cross because of everything that has overshadowed it. There's that quote from Churchill I mentioned earlier, about how a medal glitters but it also casts a shadow. This is a case in point: the shine had gone, lost in the shadows of the accusations that followed.

I was worried, too, for my own safety and that of my family. Once your name was out in public, then there was the potential for you to be made a target. That wasn't just a theoretical concern. Back when Danny Boy happened and the awards were announced, some of the soldiers in the regiment gave interviews to the press. A short while later, there had been a police raid on a suspected terror target. In the property that they raided, they found a list of names and potential targets, among which was one of the soldiers who'd been interviewed. He was moved to a safe house as a result.

So I was well aware of that when the details about the inquiry became public. I triple-locked the doors at night. Each evening, I'd do a 5-and-20 check. This was standard army procedure: you do a walk around the perimeter at 5 and 20 metres, looking out for any wires or anything else unusual. I was using my army training to protect my family. It was just a precaution, but when it came to those I loved, I felt I couldn't be too careful.

I always thought I wouldn't be called. Everyone else who was with me that day, all their stories were going to be slightly different because everyone has got a different perspective on things. I get that. But there was nothing in those differences, everyone who was in that team was on the same page and knew that nothing like the suggested allegations had happened. No, I thought. They aren't going to fucking want to see me. I thought that there was nothing in my statement which would give anyone an idea to then call me in and put me on the stand.

The solicitors were on our side, but at the same time they did not make me feel that everything was going to be all right. I knew they were doing their job, being cautious, because you just never know. But at least they were present. The only time I saw any representation from the MoD was actually in the inquiry room itself. I remember her shaking my fucking hand and saying, 'Oh, I am here from the MoD.' And I thought, Where the fuck have you been all this time then? I am just about to go in for my hearing, she is introducing herself to me and I am thinking, Yeah. Cheers. I don't know if that was the MoD keeping a bit of distance in case there was anything in the allegations? But as far as I was concerned, they should be there supporting. They should have been there from start to finish. The feeling I had was one of betrayal. We were sent out there, no questions asked. We believed in what the politicians were saying. We went, we worked hard, we came back, this was put out there and no one was really interested in the welfare of everyone who was involved.

While this was going on, I went out on that final tour to Afghanistan. To an outsider, that might seem a really odd decision. If the allegations are serious enough for a public inquiry, how can these soldiers still be sent out on tour? At the time, I just thought, I am going away on an operational tour, this is what I joined for. I have got a job to do and I have to do that to the best of my ability. But, looking back, I do think how did they allow me to go? And it wasn't just me. Stick Broom, who was my commander in Iraq, he went operational too. He did two tours of Afghan. Rushforth, he went on another, he went on Telic 8 which was pretty punchy. They were happy to question our decision-making on the battlefield but still fine for us to crack on and go away on more tours.

In the army itself, no one really talked about the inquiry. No one would bring it up because when you are going operational you are so in tune to working with your men. The senior officers could have been thinking, Fucking hell, he's already going through it, is he in the right state of mind to be out here? But I was unaware of it. I think I might have had the odd couple of conversations with other soldiers, the gist of which was, *This is bollocks. This is shit.* But what else could I do? I just had to get on with it. And that is kind of what I did.

After that first contact about the public inquiry, the letters kept coming. It was a real drip, drip, drip of requests, going over statements and clarifying this comment or that. I found myself getting frustrated and wound up. Every time I tried to switch off, shut all those memories down, another letter would arrive on the doorstep.

Every question was like the flicking of a switch. I'm only human, so as soon as I got a letter asking me to recollect a particular detail, I was right back there. I found myself revisiting Danny Boy again and again. It's a horrible feeling to have to go back through all of that. It was something I didn't discuss with Lucy, with my dad or anyone. Lucy was asking questions – 'Why do they keep sending you all these letters?' – but I didn't want to get into it with her. No one else could really understand it, so I'd sign what needed to be signed, send them back, then would give myself ten minutes to suck it all back in and try and get on with my life.

It wasn't just the lawyers. Because I'd done a couple of pieces before, and I was known because of the Military Cross, I was getting contacted by journalists as well. And not just me – they tracked down my brother in Scotland. How they got his address I've no idea, but they turned up on his doorstep and asked him what he thought about it all. He shut the door on them pretty quickly.

And that was what I was still trying to do with the inquiry as well. As much as I could, I was shutting it out. I wasn't following it on the news, or going on the Internet to find out what was going on. I had a date from my solicitors as to when I was likely to appear and that was enough for me. I asked them the question, what would happen if I was found guilty? Would I be stripped of my decoration? Their answer was that it was complicated – because it was an inquiry rather than a trial, nothing would happen from my cross-examination. But if the inquiry did somehow decide I was guilty of the claims being made, then that would open me up to the possibility of prosecution. And manslaughter, or whatever those charges might be, would lead to prison.

From my perspective, it felt like everything good we had achieved was being forgotten about. That was all in the shadows now, under the weight of these accusations.

There were moments in the process when I started to doubt myself. I had to go back through my statements and that led me to wonder if I'd got all the details right. One of them was the number of POWs we escorted in the back of the Warrior when we returned to camp. I had different numbers in the statements – three in one, four in another. The more I thought about it, I wasn't sure. It was so long ago, it was dark in the back of the vehicle and there was so much other stuff going on I simply couldn't be completely certain. My lawyers asked me if I wanted to change my statement, but I didn't want to. If that was what I'd said in the first place, then I'd stick to that. If people were suspicious, it was only going to look more suspicious if I started to change the details at this stage.

I just wanted it all to go away, to get it over with and focus back on where I was and what I was doing now. But that wasn't easy to do. As the day for my appearance at the inquiry got closer, I was increasingly preoccupied by it.

My appearance was scheduled for Monday 4 November 2013. I was serving in Germany at the time, which was a bit of a blessing. Being out there made it a bit easier to be away from it all. Out of sight and all that. I flew back to the UK at the end of the previous week, so I could spend some time prepping with the lawyers for what was going to happen. I know that some of those appearing at the inquiry brought people along with them for support, but I left Lucy and my family behind, didn't ask my parents, anyone. As I'd done with pretty much all the aftermath of Danny Boy, I dealt with it by myself.

It wasn't just my family who weren't there at the inquiry. While I had meetings set up to meet my lawyers, I had no contact from anyone else. Not a single contact from the MoD, the government, anyone. As I said earlier, the first time I met anyone from the MoD to talk about the inquiry was when I was introduced to their legal representative at the hearing itself. Looking back, I find that extraordinary – no support system, no one asking if I wanted to talk to someone about it.

On the Friday before my appearance at the inquiry, I headed into central London to meet the lawyers who were going to be representing me on the Monday. That was where it all got a bit real. They talked me though the set-up and how to approach answering the questions I'd be asked. If there was anything I was uncomfortable answering, I should just say, no comment. They told me not to make my answers too long, because that was where I'd be likely to get flustered and could open myself up to harder follow-ups. *Stick to the questions, keep your answers to the facts and try not to get drawn.* They talked me through all the mannerisms to look out from the other legal team – the ways they might try to throw me off balance or provoke me.

We went through some of the questions they thought I was likely to be asked. They knew better than me what had been going on in the inquiry, so knew the potential issues that could come up. They'd gone through my statement and highlighted various sections; we talked through what my answers would be. The lawyers told me that should I feel myself getting flustered, to make sure I took a pause. Have a sip of water, catch my breath before answering. They showed me various photos, too, that were likely to come up, pictures from the battle scene. That was a bit of shock to me, there were photos from that day that I'd never seen before. Again, that brought it all back. It was a lot to take in, and the more they explained, the more nervous I got. But at least now I had a better idea of what I was going to be up against.

That weekend was a weird one. I went back to stay with Lucy's parents. I didn't tell them why I was in the UK, just that I had a military matter to attend to in London on the Monday. They didn't ask and I didn't tell, which was fine by me. I can't have been great company that weekend. I had my file and statements to go through, so I just kept my head down and went through those.

I didn't sleep well the night before. I never do in those situations. And I don't eat either, all I had for breakfast on the Monday morning was a bottle of water. It was a cold day, I remember that. I was wearing my suit with our blue-yellow-blue regimental tie and was chilly with nerves. The fact that I didn't have an overcoat on didn't help matters. I got the train into London and then the Underground to Holborn, then walked to the lawyers' offices. We'd agreed I'd meet them there, then we'd walk to where the inquiry was being held.

By now I was getting really keyed up. When we got to where the public inquiry was being held, there were press waiting outside: journalists, photographers and cameramen. We didn't stop. My lawyer ushered me straight in and it was then the butterfly nerves really kicked in. I could feel the nerves hit my stomach but I tried to keep my cool as I was ushered in. Outside the main inquiry room was a corridor with mirrored windows, allowing those outside to see in. The corridor was full of flat-screen TVs everywhere showing live feeds to the main inquiry room. This was my first glimpse of where I'd be questioned: it was a large area, with elements of a traditional courtroom but lined with desks and computers. At the top was where the chairman of the inquiry would sit, then I could see the dock where I'd be and the tables where the main lawyers would be. The rest of the main floor was filled with these desks and computers, with the press and public sat in a gallery down the side. There were people milling everywhere, a lot of bustle and movement.

Although I'd been told repeatedly this was an inquiry not a court trial, the dock looked pretty much like a dock you'd see in a courtroom: made out of light wood, boxing the person in. There was a microphone to speak into, a shelf to put your water on and that was it. It was difficult not to feel exposed sitting in that – difficult not to feel as though you were on trial.

I was taken to a holding room to wait until I was called. Eventually, it was time. I was taken in, shown into the dock. I'd defy anyone not to feel nervous in that situation, everyone looking at you, thinking goodness knows what. I tried to scan the room, work out who was going to be questioning me. But it was a sea of faces to be honest. The only people I recognised I could count on one hand. There was Neil Sheldon, who was the lawyer assigned to represent military witnesses in the inquiry. There was Melanie Cumberland, the MoD lawyer, who had introduced herself to me as I was waiting to go in.

And there was Phil Shiner. I knew who he was because he had been in the press talking about the inquiry, so I recognised him from that – he had these distinctive little glasses with coloured rims. He just sat there, a presence in the room, watching, observing what was going on. If I was worried before, seeing him there doubled down on those nerves.

But I didn't have much time to think. I was ushered into the dock, then the room stood for the arrival of the inquiry chairman, Sir Thayne Forbes. There was no going back now. This was it – the moment of truth.

CHAPTER SEVENTEEN

ON THE STAND

'**GOOD MORNING, COLOUR SERGEANT.** I am the chairman of this Public Inquiry to whom you will be giving your evidence. I just want to take a few moments to confirm with you the procedure that we will be following ...'

Sir Thayne Forbes was a former High Court judge. He was clearly a serious guy, but there was something about his demeanour that immediately helped to put me more at ease. You know when you look at someone and face-to-face you get a sense of them? It felt like that. He came across as thoughtful and fair-minded, which was all I could have asked for.

'This is, as you know, an Inquiry,' he continued. 'It is not a trial. However, I have decided as a matter of principle that all the witnesses should give their evidence on oath, or affirm to tell the truth when giving evidence.'

That all sounded a bit more serious to me – if it wasn't a trial, why was I giving evidence under oath? Despite his words, that sort of statement made it difficult not to feel you were in a courtroom setting. Sat in that box with everyone looking up at you, it was almost impossible not to feel under pressure. It was daunting. Given the choice, I would have much rather been out fighting than being sat in that dock. I felt I was under more pressure in an inquiry room than when I was a commander out in the field.

The chairman explained how my evidence consisted of two parts: the written witness statements I'd already put forward and the answers to the questions I was about to give. 'You will be asked by a number of lawyers who are present here in the hearing room this morning and who represent various different interests at this Inquiry.'

He went on to introduce the lawyers, one by one. 'The first of those lawyers is Mr Beer, the gentleman standing in the centre of the room. He is Counsel to the Inquiry itself. He will be asking you questions on behalf of the Inquiry; in effect, he will be asking questions on my behalf. He will be the lawyer who will ask you most of the questions that you will be asked this morning.'

This first lawyer, Jason Beer, was a bit difficult to read. Looking at him across the inquiry room, he didn't seem either overtly friendly or aggressive. There was a bit of the poker-face going on: controlled, professional. But I liked the chairman and if Beer was the chairman's man, then I hoped that meant he would be all right.

'I have agreed that lawyers representing other interests should have an opportunity to ask you some questions on a much more limited basis,' the chairman continued. 'The first of those additional lawyers will be one who appears on behalf of the Iraqi core participants. They are the families and the relatives of the various Iraqis who died during the course of the incidents with which we are concerned and also the various Iraqis who were detained during the course of the same incidents.'

If Jason Beer was asking the questions on the chairman's behalf, then this second lawyer, Steven Powles, was quizzing me on behalf of Phil Shiner. And if I'd taken an immediate liking to the chairman, I felt the exact opposite with Steven Powles. He had an attitude and presence, slicked-back hair and a bit of smugness to him. There was something about him that irritated me right away.

'He will be followed by a lawyer who may ask some questions on behalf of the Ministry of Defence,' the chairman continued. This was Melanie Cumberland, the MoD lawyer who I'd only just met. 'Finally, you may be asked some questions by the lawyer who represents the vast majority of the military witnesses at this Inquiry' – this was my lawyer, Neil Sheldon. At least he is going to be on my side, I remember thinking. If he ends up not asking me many questions, then I'll know I've done okay. But there were a lot of obstacles to get past before I got to him.

The first step was to stand and take the affirmation – I'm not massively religious, so it made more sense than being sworn in. That shouldn't have made me nervous – all I was doing was confirming I was going to tell the truth, which I was – but it had that courtroom feel that set me on edge. Even when you've nothing to hide, it's difficult to be in that set-up, with everyone watching you, and not feel a little worried. I took the affirmation, then sat back down and waited for Jason Beer to start.

'Can you take out the binder that's in front of you?' he asked, gesturing towards the blue folder I had with me in the dock. He asked me to turn to the last page of my witness statement, where I'd signed it. 'Is that your signature?' he asked. 'Are the contents of that statement true?'

'They are, yes.'

Beer went on to ask me a series of general questions, about when I joined the army, what my rank was, when I'd been deployed to Iraq and so forth. It was all stuff that he must have known already, I guess he was asking just to ease me in a bit. But I must have been sounding quiet or nervous, because after a handful of questions he said after one answer, 'If you just move slightly forwards to the microphone.' I tried to lean forwards but went too far: 'Without getting too close,' he corrected, and I shuffled back again a bit, feeling a little uncertain of myself.

'Can I turn to the afternoon of 14 May, please?'

Now the preamble was over. Beer asked me what we'd been doing in the run-up to the Danny Boy incident.

'I remember being on a VCP,' I answered, 'vehicle checkpoint, just doing the normal daily routine of pulling over a certain amount of vehicles per day. And I particularly remember Sergeant Broome being quite animated with his hand signals and the signal was basically to mount up. So it was just a fist in the air and a circle motion and that was the signal to mount up, so I ...'

'Just stopping there, Colour Sergeant,' Beer interrupted me. 'So you were actually out on the ground when the tasking arrived to attend the incident which became known as the Danny Boy ...'

'That's right,' I said, surprised that he'd picked me up on this.

'So you don't remember being back at camp and getting a message to help some Argylls that had been caught in an ambush?'

'No.'

'Okay. You were actually out on the ground already?'

'Yes,' I replied. That exchange unnerved me. Such a small detail, yet he'd asked me about it again, and then again. Was I right about that? That was my recollection, so what else could I say? There was no comeback – my responses were just noted and the questioning moved on.

'If you look at the screen to your right there, Colour Sergeant.' Beer pointed over to a TV screen where a photograph was brought up. 'This is a photograph taken at about 5.28 – 17.28 – on the day. Do you recognise either of the soldiers in that photograph?'

Having the photograph put up there was a shock. It felt a bit like they were pulling the carpet from under me, bringing up something that I'd never seen before. I thought I'd done the prep, but we were barely a few minutes into the questioning and we were going off down a route I hadn't been prepared for. I remembered what my lawyer had said in the briefing, and told myself to pause, count to three in my head, take a sip of water before answering. Cigar moment.

'No,' I replied. 'I've not seen these, to be honest, this particular photograph, but what I can tell you now is the gentleman on the right is carrying a light support weapon. The only person to carry a light support weapon in my Warrior was Tatawaqa.'

'And that's not Tatawaqa?'

I shook my head. 'The left-hand gentleman, I think, is Corporal Byles due to the chest-rig that he's wearing there.'

Beer asked me how I knew that. 'That's tailor-made,' I explained. 'It's a bit more Gucci-er bit of kit.'

Beer looked at me blankly. 'You have to explain that word.'

Gucci-er was an army term. Some people would amend their kit to make it better than the standard-issue stuff we were given; tailoring it is something we did to make the kit more comfortable or so that you could get to your field dressings or medical kit faster, or whatever. Looking good is important in the military. So making your kit Gucci-er, or Ally-er, as it is sometimes called, is a thing. It's all fairly standard stuff, the term a bit of army banter, but as I explained it to the complete silence of the inquiry room, that didn't really come across.

Beer continued to question me as to our whereabouts before the incident, where we were when the call came in about the ambush. All of this had been covered in my statement, but he asked me anyway, presumably to set the scene. *Could I remember where I was when the tasking came in? No. Was it on Route 6? Yes. Did you travel south on Route 6? I don't know. Did you travel towards Danny Boy?* By the time he asked me that last question, I could feel myself getting irritated. You know I fucking did, I thought. I was involved in the Battle of Danny Boy. But you can't answer like that. You have to keep your composure. So I just answered yes and we moved on.

'Okay,' Beer said. He said 'okay' a lot and a lot of them were those 'okay's where you weren't quite sure how okay he thought your answer actually was. 'What was the next thing to happen as you travelled towards Danny Boy?'

'I just remember the vehicle coming to a halt and the sound of heavy incoming fire.'

'Was that the sound of the discharge of weapons,' Beer asked, 'or was it the sound of ordnance hitting the vehicle or both?'

'Yeah, both.'

'What was that? Was it small arms fire or anything other than small arms fire?'

'It was small arms fire and – the RPGs, the grenades.'

There were a lot of questions like this, this sort of point-by-point legal unpicking of all the details. The difference between me and him was that I was someone experienced in combat situations. I'd been in these situations far too often, so I knew quite clearly what it was I'd been hearing. But I'd give him my answer, he'd ask again and I'd give him the same answer again. I couldn't read what he was after. Was he after a different answer to the one I was giving him?

The questions felt as though I was walking through a minefield. Beer asked me about our vehicle returning fire. 'To which direction was it engaging? Left, right, straight on?'

'It was right,' I replied. 'I do know in my statement I have said left, but it was – it was to the right-hand side.'

'I think there you are referring to your first Royal Military Police statement – is that right?'

'Yes.'

'Is that incorrect?'

I've just said that, haven't I?

'That is incorrect, yes.'

'Okay,' said Beer.

The way he was questioning, it was making me out as though I couldn't tell left from right. But I was in the back of the Warrior, all but pitch black with just a tiny glass hole to see out of, and that had condensation on it. And not only could I see next to nothing, but I was sat there with my adrenaline pumping. I was about to go out into the unknown. I wasn't thinking, Is that left or right, but, Am I going to survive?

'Can you recall, moving forward a little bit, when you got out of the vehicle, whether there was a factory?'

'I do remember a factory.'

'Was that to the left- or the right-hand side?'

'I think it was to the left-hand side, but I don't know.'

Beer gave me a look. 'You can't remember. Okay.'

Inside, I was beginning to fume. I was being quizzed by a lawyer who'd never been in the sort of situation I'd been in or been under that sort of pressure. When you take in all the factors of what we were facing, it was a whole different ball game. One hundred per cent. And he was going on about whether I was getting out on the left or the right of the vehicle. Did it fucking matter? The important point was that we were going towards the enemy forces.

In that inquiry room, I felt belittled, humiliated. I was having my experiences taken apart by someone who did not understand battlefield awareness, battlefield confusion. At the point I was getting out of the vehicle, I was deafened by the Challenger 2 battle tank which had turned up and was firing its main armament – 120 millimetre HESH (high explosive squash head). Our vehicle's chain was going off. The main armament from the Warrior was firing. I couldn't hear anything. I was confused. My adrenaline was all over the place. The whole experience is an out-of-body one. So to ask me pointless questions on what I did and didn't remember on my surroundings, I just thought, Fucking behave.

The same was true over his questions on the use of bayonets. Beer quoted a line from my statement, where
Sergeant Broome gave me the order, 'Woody, get the
blokes prepped.' 'What does that mean?' Beer asked. So I
explained: 'Just make sure their kit is fitted, you know,
and they are all good to go, because being in a Warrior
in the middle of summer in the Iraq heat, it is [close] to
boiling point.'

Fixing bayonets on your rifle, it was SOP. It is a close-
quarter battle drill. If you are going out there and closing
with the enemy, you fix a bayonet. If you don't, you're
not doing your drills right. It is a tradition as an infantry
soldier that you do that, because what happens if you
approach the enemy position and you get a stoppage or
run out of ammunition? You use your bayonet. It is procedure, you do it time and again in training – no big
deal. But the fact that Beer would focus on it, it just suggested a lack of understanding of what the situation was
really like.

'There is a quote attributed to you on a BBC website,'
Beer continued, 'it is said that you said, "We've got a lot of
firepower with a Warrior, so I'd never dreamt we would be
told to dismount and engage in close-quarter battles. It
hadn't happened since the Falklands War."' He paused. 'Is
that something that you said to a journalist?'

'Maybe words to that effect,' I replied, 'but clearly journalists will be journalists.'

I was being honest there. I probably did say that. But I didn't like him linking the two up – suggesting that what was SOP was in fact something highly unusual.

'Does it follow that the order to dismount into the battle rather surprised you?' Beer asked.

'That's what we do,' I replied. 'We're infantry soldiers, so we train to close with and destroy the enemy. So it was just a shock because it's not every day you get an order like that.'

The questioning moved on to the dismount, but the querying of specifics continued. Beer brought up on the screen a diagram I'd drawn of the incident. He started asking about irrigation ditches and whether I remember it being U- or V-shaped. He asked about timings, as though I was checking my watch every couple of minutes. I didn't have a working radio, that dropped its fill as soon as I left the Warrior, so I wasn't getting instructions or information from them. The more he asked, the more my 'yes' and 'no' responses were being mixed up with 'I don't know's and 'I can't remember's.

Beer was interested in how many people we were receiving fire from. 'Like I said in my statement, there was a couple of people which I had seen either extract to take up positions or withdraw. I had seen people leave that first position. So I said in my statement, I think, six – six to eight people, which I, today, still believe that.' Beer wanted certainty so he could follow up: So where did this person go? What did you do with him? But again, it was a line of questioning based on a misunderstanding of what a wartime situation is like. No one there could be 100 per cent certain of what happened. And everyone's recollections were different in some way or other.

That was apparent in the discussion over the approach to the first trench. My recollection was that while Rushforth, Tatawaqa and I had moved together as a three, it was Rushforth and me alone who approached the first trench. Beer queried that, saying 'Private Rushforth's recollection is that all three of you went over the top into the ditch at the same time, i.e. you, him and Tatawaqa. That's not your recollection?'

I parried back: 'It's a long time ago so he may be right.'

Then he asked me if I fired my weapon. I hadn't. He asked if anyone else had. Again I said no, only for Beer to challenge that: 'In a previous account, Corporal Byles has described that automatic fire was used on approaching and entering the trench. He has said that himself and the other lance corporal – I think that would be you – "sprung up and identified the biggest threat to us, which was neutralised by bursts of automatic fire". Is that incorrect?'

I felt awkward. The questioning was putting me in direct conflict with what a commander on the battlefield remembered. Either I changed what I said or I contradicted his account. But I knew that I had never gone into that position with Byles. I worked as a three, he worked as a pair; we were in different command roles in the same team. My memory was that automatic fire had been fired somewhere, but not by me or those I was with. So I stuck with what I remembered. 'That is incorrect,' I replied to Beer. 'That didn't happen.'

Beer then put my citation up on the screen. Not to praise what I'd done but to find differences in the account there and my own written statement. He read out a line he was particularly interested in: 'Bayonets were fixed and automatic fire used.'

'Did you fix a bayonet?' he asked.

'No,' I replied.

'Could you have fixed a bayonet on your weapon?'

'No.'

'Why was that?'

'Because it was an underslung grenade launcher,' I explained.

'Did you see Privates Rushforth and Tatawaqa fix bayonets?'

'No. Tatawaqa couldn't fix a bayonet because he had a light support weapon.'

'This whole "fix bayonets",' I tried to explain again, 'it's just standard.'

'Did you see either Byles or Beggs fix their bayonets?'

'I didn't take any notice, to be honest.'

I wouldn't have taken any notice of Rushforth and the others who fixed bayonets. There was so much going on I didn't have time to micromanage individual drills. But I guess Beer, like the media, found the idea of bayonets intriguing – hand-to-hand combat stuff. Whereas for those out in the field, it was far more routine.

More discrepancies in the different statements were dissected. Beer had this routine of asking me a question – 'Did you see any dead bodies in the trench at this point?' – then when I said no, he'd immediately bring up the statement that said the opposite.

'Sergeant Broome has told the Inquiry that he saw two dead men in the wadi, as he described it, with the four prisoners,' Beer responded. 'Private Tatawaqa I think is going to tell the Inquiry – he certainly does in his statement – that there were dead bodies around amongst the prisoners. You didn't see them at that stage?'

In the cold light of the inquiry room, the heat of the battle was difficult to explain. But I continued to try: 'No, there were clearly dead bodies, but it was – I can't remember them being in and around that first position because there was a threat which … immediate threat which I had to deal with, and that was the POWs and arresting them and going through that procedure. My main effort was to deal with the immediate threat, which was still armed and still a violent enemy.' Everyone has their own focus in that situation. I was concentrating on the people still alive, as they were the ones who might kill me.

One of those Iraqis was particularly animated. He was standing up and shouting in Arabic. He was being particularly animated with his hands. Beer asked me whether that was what he called the 'classic surrender pose'.

'So he was surrendering?' he asked.

'Yes,' I agreed, 'but very animated with that surrender.'

'Did you shout back at him something along the lines of '"Put your fucking hands up"?'

It felt weird, Beer quoting what I'd said out in the field in front of those lawyers. Like being caught swearing at school.

'Something along the lines, yes,' I admitted. Beer knew full well I'd said it, because it was in my original statement. He read that back out to the room.

'"I shouted, 'Put your fucking hands up,'" he quoted. '"At this they all put their hands up and stood up."' Beer looked up from reading the statement. 'Is that right, the other ones stood up?'

I was getting confused from the intensity of the questions. I was certain, but now the way he was phrasing it, I was less sure. My focus had been on the animated guy, the others not so much.

'I can't remember now,' I said, trying to be as honest as I could.

Beer paused. 'Do you have any reason to doubt what's in your statement?'

What kind of question was that? I felt pummelled. It was as though Beer had tried to soften me up with his other questions, picking away at my answers by knocking them back with the other accounts of the battle. Now came the kicker. 'Do you have any reason to doubt what's in your statement?' I might not have been a lawyer but I could understand what it was he was insinuating. I took a pause, a sip of water and came back.

'The reason why I say that is because now I am a little bit older and more wiser,' I reasoned. 'We would still be in massive threat with their weapons by their side, so it would have made sense for us to ask them to stand up or to make sure they stood up and away from their weapons systems.'

I thought it was a good answer. Thoughtful and reasoned. Being straight. But Beer didn't come back on it, or retract what he'd suggested. Instead, that question may have been placed there to set up what he asked next.

'The prisoner that was stood up, what did you do in relation to him?'

'I had a verbal exchange with him.' I thought back to the situation. Tried to explain it as best I could. 'I had my right hand on my weapon system and then I put my hand on his shoulder because we had come under an engagement. Whether it was our Warriors started to fire or we started to come under contact again, I just heard an engagement. So my own – my safety and the POWs, I then basically wrestled him to the ground, as in my left hand on his right shoulder, put him to the ground out of that contact situation.'

I looked at Beer. I knew exactly what he was going to ask me next. Back in Iraq, in a battle situation, there was no fucking about. You hear engagements and you are getting down. There was no time for niceties – 'Excuse me Sir, would you mind lying down?' – you just got both of you to the floor as quickly as possible. That was for his benefit as well as for yours. Not that the inquiry saw it that way.

'So you wrestled the first of them to the ground?' Beer asked.

'Yes.'

'Did you strike him in any way?'

For God's sake. 'No.'

'Did you kick him in any way?'

'No.'

'Did you use your weapon to strike him in any way?'

'No.'

As far as I was concerned, I'd been saving this guy's life. A grab and a pull to get him to safety. But for Beer, it seemed to be potential evidence of brutality. And he had the claims to back this up.

'Sergeant Webb, a member of the RMP, has given the Inquiry a statement that later that day he was told that a lance corporal kicked one of the detainees down into cover because "there" – i.e. the lance corporal's position – was under fire. Did you speak with a Sergeant Webb later that day from the RMP?'

Webb must have been one of the Military Police, but I couldn't remember speaking to him. 'I can't remember who I spoke to that day.'

Beer rephrased the question. 'Did you tell anyone subsequently that you kicked one of the detainees down into cover because your position was under fire?'

'No.' I hadn't and I wouldn't have done. I didn't have time to mess around and start kicking anyone about. I just put him to the ground as quickly as I could to get us both safe.

Beer continued. 'Corporal Byles has told the Inquiry that in the ditch he hit the men with his fists and the back of his rifle to get them to surrender. Did you see him do that?'

I hadn't. Beers asked me about an article in the *Sun* where Byles is quoted as saying 'I bayonet people, I slashed people.' I hadn't seen him do anything like that myself. Indeed, when Byles was interviewed for the Inquiry he denied ever speaking to the *Sun* or making those statements.

Beer's implication throughout this exchange was how we'd mistreated the Iraqis. I don't know what Byles did with his bayonet, but for all Beer's insinuations, it would have been good drill if he had used it. If he felt his life was in danger, then that is what an infantry soldier is trained to do, to close with and destroy the enemy. I felt like saying to Beer, 'You know these were enemy fighters we were dealing with? They weren't farmers or civvies. These were militia fighters who we were up against: some of them were young guys with the bit between their teeth; others were ingrained, experienced, savvy.'

In that situation, you don't mess about. Your body is full of adrenaline, you feel totally pumped. And when you are fighting for your life, you'll do whatever it takes to make sure you stay alive. The situation that Beer was unpicking was one of chaos. There is so much to think about and process and you're trying to do all that and keep calm and ensure you don't freeze in the moment; the thought of some sort of premeditated brutality just doesn't come into the equation. Once you start getting angry or letting your emotions run over, then you've lost it. You've got to keep your head, as the poem says.

Anything else was counterproductive. If people you were dealing with thought they were under threat, or at risk, then who knows how they might respond. What was going through my head in that trench was not just getting the weapons cleared, but whether these fighters had grenades hidden under their bellies. What happened before was that fighters would undo the pin and safety clip, lie on top of the grenade and then, when you rolled them over, it would go off. There is so much to think about in those split seconds of conflict that you're concentrating on getting the important stuff right. Looking back, we achieved our aim, because we all survived. Was it a textbook operation? Of course not, but we did our best in circumstances that were chaotic and messy. That should be more than enough, you shouldn't have your split-second life-or-death decisions picked apart.

Beer asked me about my dealings with the fighter I'd pulled to ground. 'I thought he was the biggest threat,' I explained. 'The others were calm ... they were happy to follow orders, where this individual was just not very happy at all.' Beer asked me about the other detainees, but I couldn't remember. 'This is what I was going to elaborate,' I said. 'When you are fixated with a male on male, you know, that takes my attention away from anyone else. So it's trying to get him calm, detained and searched, and it's a lot of effort, especially when someone is not wanting to do that.'

Beer switched tack, from comparing my statements with those of the other soldiers to the claims made by the Iraqi militia. He asked me about Tatawaqa – *Did you see him use any force in relation to the prisoners? Did you see him hit any of the prisoners? Did you see him kick any of the prisoners?* When I answered no to each of the questions, Beer said that 'a man call Mahdi Al-Behadili, who was subsequently given the detainee number 773, alleges that a black soldier punched him on the nose, causing it to break. I think it must be Private Tatawaqa who that allegation refers to. Did you see that happen?'

I hadn't and I wasn't sure about his question either. Beggs is black as well, I pointed out. That seemed to throw Beer off track. He rephrased his question, asking whether Beggs or Tatawaqa had punched al-Behadili. But my answer was still the same.

What I wanted to say was that if either of them had broken this guy's nose, I wouldn't have blamed them for doing so. I was switched on enough not to say that, but it was what I felt. You do what you feel is the right thing to take away the threat to your life. These people have been trying to kill you. So if someone crunched them on the nose and broke it, that is fucking minor compared to what they were trying to do to us.

The accusations continued. Al-Behadili alleged that he was kicked more than twice while blindfolded and cuffed on the floor. A second detainee, Kadhim al-Behadili, said that soldiers pushed his head hard on to the ground with a hand on his neck, stepped on the back of his knees and dragged him across the ground by his ankles. A third detainee alleged a black soldier had kicked him in the chest, punched him twice on the jaw and struck him on the head with a rifle. A fourth detainee said a black soldier punched him repeatedly in the face then he was kicked by a number of soldiers until he lost consciousness.

I'd seen nothing of the sort and told Beer so. The specifics of the claims made me suspicious. I was sat there being careful and measured with my answers, all couched in what I could and couldn't recall, yet here the accusations were, in crystal-clear detail. It was all a fucking bluff. Nothing of that sort happened. If anything of that sort had happened, it would have been stopped straight off. On a purely practical level, there simply wasn't the time. The battlefield wasn't cleared. Would professional soldiers really risk their lives filling people in when the enemy was still out there? It just wouldn't happen. And it didn't happen. So having these questions and accusations thrown about me and my men, it really got to me.

Beer asked me about the plasticuffing of the prisoners: 'You say in your statement that the SOP in relation to handcuffing is to check for tightness by grabbing the plasticuff and shaking it. Is that right?'

'You would make sure it's loose enough by putting your thumb in ... you would put your thumb in and just make sure it's loosened enough. You would not put it in and then drag it round. You would give it a shake to make sure that there is enough flexibility in that wrist that's not going to stop the circulation.'

'Did you check any of the handcuffs for tightness?' Beer asked. 'Can you recall whether anyone else did? Did you see any injuries caused by the application of handcuffs?'

'I can't remember,' I replied. 'I can't remember. No.'

In the inquiry room, my answers sounded evasive. But no soldier would remember that, it's such a small detail. Someone would have been told to plasticuff the detainees and that would have been it. You wouldn't have thought about it again. Inside, I was thinking, Fucking shut it up. Why are we even discussing this? I am a British soldier and you are a British person as a British citizen questioning me about how I applied a plasticuff when I am out fighting for my country, protecting and serving this great nation. What the fuck is all this about? You cuff them so they are not going to use their hands, so they can't pull a fast one. If it's a bit tight, well, tough shit.

'Can you recall them being blindfolded?' Beer asked.

Beer knew full well that the prisoners had been blindfolded. I explained to him that we used clothing they were wearing, shemaghs and mine tape. The way he was questioning, it again sounded as though we were mistreating them by doing this, when in fact it was all standard procedure. The system with POWs is that you disarm, disorientate and you maintain that shock of capture. That was what we had been trained to do before we went to Iraq and that was exactly what we carried out. There were security reasons for blindfolding them as well. We didn't want them coming into the camp, seeing the layout and then getting word back for the next time someone wanted to send a mortar attack in. We didn't sandbag the prisoners or anything like that. We'd have used goggles if we'd had any, but we didn't, so had to adapt to what we had and used clothing to do it.

I remember glancing across at Melanie Cumberland, the MoD lawyer, and at Neil Sheldon, the lawyer who was there to represent me. Come on guys, I thought. Why aren't you stepping in? What the discussion needed was someone to intervene and say, 'Look, can we just put this whole dis-cussion into context? This is standard military procedure that Brian is being grilled about here. These guys in the field aren't doing anything they haven't been taught or instructed to do.' But instead, I was there, on my own, defending army policy.

No one else in that room had been a front-line soldier. And that made the discussion difficult. Without that expe-rience, how could you properly understand what we'd been faced with? It's not hard to sit in an air-conditioned inquiry room and make comments about blindfolds and plasticuffs and insinuate that our behaviour was brutal and barbaric. But the lack of understanding of being in that situation, the context of how the army carries out its instructions, that I did find shocking.

War isn't a contract negotiation. You're not sat there, dotting every last 'i' and crossing every last 't' until agree-ment is reached. You're under threat. You're under fire. Your life is in danger. You rely on gut and instinct to get through, do what you have to do in order to survive. That's the basics of what being a soldier is all about. That's what it felt as though I was defending. And that's what I felt as though no one in that inquiry room properly understood.

CHAPTER EIGHTEEN

WATER

AFTER AN HOUR or so of this grilling, the chairman called for a short break. I needed one. I was taken back out to the holding room and I asked if I could use the toilet. I was escorted there, the guy standing guard outside. I don't know if it was procedure, or whether they wanted to make sure I didn't use my phone or try to contact anyone. But it was disconcerting. Again, for all the talk that this wasn't a trial, having someone on guard when you went to the loo suggested otherwise.

Back in the holding room, my lawyer Neil Sheldon was waiting for me.

'How am I doing?' I asked.

'Really good,' he told me. 'Just keep doing what you're doing.' Neil told me not to hold on to the questions, as he put it. That's what the lawyers wanted, for me to start talking away and give them the opportunity to take apart what I said. Keep it simple, stick to the straight answers and I'd make it through.

At this point, the end of the session felt a long way away. I felt really frustrated at how the questioning was going. All the scrutiny was suggesting that I'd done something wrong. I knew I hadn't, but under that barrage it was easy to start thinking, But did I? When I went back into the inquiry room, I clocked Steven Powles sitting there. He was sat there, straight up, waiting for his turn to get to me. I wasn't looking forward to that.

Beer, though, was far from finished with me. He began the second session by showing a number of photos taken from inside and outside of the Warrior. One of the photos was of four detainees. I'd said in my statement that I recognised one of them because he was a little bit chubbier than the others: 'male one was about 6 feet tall of a fat build. He was wearing a blue T-shirt, black trousers and flip-flops.'

I left it at that, but I recognised this guy for another reason. He was that policeman, one of the Iraqis that we'd been training. I'd mentored him in our skills and drills, taken him through the procedures of how we searched vehicles, all in preparation for the eventual handover of tasks to the Iraqi forces. Instead, he was standing there in front of me, waffling away in Arabic. You fucking Judas, I thought. You turncoat. He didn't even have the guts to look guilty. He knew who I was, but didn't give a fuck. And that, in a way, summed up a lot of my feelings about this whole charade. Here we were, doing our best to help the Iraqis get their country back in order, make it stable again; here they were, taking advantage of that training and then attacking us and claiming we'd mistreated them.

Beer brought up another photo. This one was of me, Byles, Broome and Tatawaqa. Tatawaqa had his thumb up.

'Now this appears to be a posed photograph,' Beer said. 'Would you agree?'

I agreed. Looking back, it was the wrong thing to have done. I think we were pumped at having survived, someone stuck a camera in our face and we'd responded. But there was a world of difference between that and taking a trophy photograph, which was what Beer suggested.

Beer focused on Tatawaqa. 'Do you see that he has what appears to be red knuckles?' he asked. 'You didn't see him get bloody knuckles from punching someone?'

Again, Beer didn't really get it. He'd got the accusation from the Iraqi about being hit in the face, he'd got what appeared to be red on Tatawaqa's knuckles, put two and two together and made five. This was a war zone, not a crime scene. There were bodies and casualties who had been hit by some pretty powerful ordnance: 30-millimetre rounds, which cause some serious damage if they hit you. If you are hit, you are opened up. We had to move what was left of these bodies, and without gloves. There was blood everywhere, we had it on our chests and hands and legs. What did that mean? That we'd kneed them in the face as well?

I was quizzed about Sergeant Major Falconer and I heading over to clear and secure the other trenches. Or more specifically, the accounts that Falconer and I had given about what happened. This time, Beer was less interested in the differences between the two accounts, but more in the similarities.

'Do you remember when you made this statement you gave it to a Sergeant Webb of the RMP?' Beer held up the original statement I'd given after Danny Boy. 'If we just look at the last page ... it is counter-signed by Sergeant Webb.' Beer went on. 'Do you remember that at the same time Sergeant Major Falconer was in the same room as you and he was having his statement taken by another RMP Sergeant, Sergeant Tucker?' If the suggestion wasn't clear, he rephrased it. 'Can you remember the circumstances in which your statements were taken, i.e. you were in a room at the same time, one person perhaps at one desk and one person at another, each with an RMP sergeant?'

My immediate response to Beer's question was, *Why would you even do that? How could you concentrate to give a statement when someone else was in the same room as you?* The only thing I could remember about Falconer and that statement was him coming in to have a go at Webb. 'This is beyond a joke', he told him, 'we are at war here, we've just come back from being out on the ground for eight hours and you've got Woody in, asking him for statements.'

Maybe this was being naive. Because as Beer continued his questioning, I realised what he was driving at: that Falconer and I had somehow colluded on our statements, to make sure the details matched up. Falconer's statement said that he'd shot at six Iraqi fighters in total. But in my second statement in August 2004, which Beer then brought up, I'd said that we'd killed two enemy soldiers.

'As I have said already,' Beer concluded. 'Sergeant Major Falconer describes engaging three lots of two enemy dead. You don't recall that at all?'

'No,' I replied.

'It's not the case you were, in August 2004, minimising the number of dead that you and Sergeant Major Falconer shot?'

This was bullshit. Beer was concocting some sort of conspiracy between me and Falconer over what we told the RMP, reaching for something that simply wasn't there. He went back to my original statement I'd given immediately after Danny Boy and picked through the discrepancies. In the August statement, I'd described how Falconer and I had moved about 150 metres when someone had jumped from a trench 20 metres in front of us with an AK-47; Falconer had dropped him. Then I'd seen another enemy combatant to my left, aiming an RPG in our direction. I'd engaged him.

That detail hadn't been included in the original statement, as Beer was eager to point out. 'In this statement you don't describe the incident where somebody was bringing an RPG into line to fire and you engaging them and the other person that Sergeant Major Falconer engaged and "dropped" as you put it. Is there any reason for that?'

For all my lawyer's advice of keeping calm and keeping it simple, I couldn't contain myself. I wasn't going to let him get away with these suggestions. So what were the reasons behind the statements being different? Collusion? Cover-up? My response was short and sharp.

'RMP not doing their job properly?'

That was the truth. Those first statements were a bit of a shambles. We were tired and under pressure. Getting those statements done was not a priority. In the light of day now, I wish we had done them properly, as it would have made all of what happened next much easier. Instead, those statements were just sketched essentially, a shorthand of what happened, which left holes for any lawyer who wanted to, to get digging. Beer, though, he had his different theory for the discrepancies.

'What about you not telling the RMP what happened?'

This all felt as though it was getting personal. He was questioning my integrity, which I really didn't like. 'The statements are pretty poor,' I came back, 'what I have read, by the RMP. I've said it in one of the statements and I don't know why it's not in that statement. There are a few other things with my statements which I've said things and they have not been in there, so I don't know. I can't answer that question.'

'There isn't any clear account in this first RMP statement of you and Sergeant Major Falconer killing, at relatively close range, two Iraqi men, is there? That's a pretty significant event, isn't it?' Beer was sticking to his point, I'd give him that. 'You can't give a reason as to why those events aren't included in the statement?'

'No,' I said. And I couldn't. The answer lay with the RMP who'd put that statement together. And it wasn't the only answer that those RMP officers needed to give.

'Sergeant Webb, the RMP interviewer,' Beer went on, 'says that he clearly recalls you telling him that you engaged with further enemies after detaining the four detainees and throwing a hand grenade into the enemy position when you initially encountered them. Is that right?'

'No,' I disagreed.

'Did you tell Sergeant Webb that?'

No I did not. I didn't tell him because no hand grenades were thrown. That was a fact.

'Just to be clear, you say that Sergeant Webb is wrong in his recollection that you told him that you had engaged further enemy by throwing a hand grenade into the enemy position?'

'Yes,' I said. 'That's totally wrong.'

How that got in there, I just don't know. I had a UGL on me, but that is a weapon system, not a hand grenade. And I didn't even fire mine anyway. It all seemed very odd, what the RMP officer was saying I'd said. And it seemed odd, too, that the inquiry was taking it so seriously. Believing second-hand, word-of-mouth stuff rather than my recollections of what had actually happened. I thought it was really off myself, bringing up stuff like that where there was no evidence, just hearsay.

Beer was really pushing my buttons now. He moved on to the clear-up, when we found weapon systems where the POWs had been.

'You say,' Beer quoted my statement, '"There were weapons next to the depression from which the two detainees emerged."'

'I've got no reason to doubt that statement.'

'That gives the impression that you knew at the point of detaining them that there were weapons next to them in the depression from which they emerged, rather than someone telling you later, "Oh, by the way, those two people that you detained, there were weapons where they stood."'

'Clearly I'm not current on my statement,' I answered back. 'That is maybe an error in judgement, that I should have read and memorised my statement off by heart, because there was so much that went on that day, you know, and it was nine years ago, as well. Yes, I have no reason to believe my statement is wrong, but also I am not 100 per cent totally current with my statement, as in reading it night after night after night.'

God knows what my lawyer thought of my answers at this point, but Beer had changed his tone and his approach and I'd kind of had enough. *I'm not having that*, I thought. Looking back, I should probably have kept my cool, but I'd hold my hat to anyone who could manage that under the sustained questioning and their derogatory implications.

Beer didn't respond to my outburst. Maybe he couldn't come back on that, or maybe he thought he'd got me. Either way he ignored it.

'Neither of them were wearing chest webbing,' he asked. 'Is that right?'

'Yes,' I replied sarcastically, repeating his question back to him, 'they weren't wearing chest webbing.'

'And you didn't actually see them holding weapons which they then dropped?'

'No.'

'Might it be,' Beer dropped his next accusation in, 'that they didn't have anything to do with the engagement?'

'What, and they just randomly had weapons?'

You're so not getting this, I thought.

'That's what I'm trying to test,' Beer tried to sound reasonable, even if his hypothesis wasn't, 'whether they did have weapons or not and how clear you are that they did have weapons that were on the floor next to them.'

I was steaming. My words started tumbling out, one over the other. 'As I said before, there was that much gone on that day and it was on the way back as well and they had come out of nowhere. I can't now sit here and say I remember physically going over and checking that position for weapons systems. One, I was just glad that I wasn't engaged by them; two, there was more enemy on that battlefield because it was a battlefield – simple and straightforward as that.'

And that was the nub of it. It was a battlefield, not a farmer's field. When you were as vulnerable as we had been to enemy fire, when you had just gone through what we had experienced and clearing more positions with the sergeant major, when you want to get back to the safety of everyone else, I was not going to go back and check if their weapons were there. That, I knew would get done in the after-process of clearing the battlefield.

Fucking clowns, I thought, looking at Beer and everyone else. You're asking me these questions when you've no idea what you're talking to me about. I remember looking across and thinking, You've got no credibility on this, none whatsoever. The accusations from the Iraqis, that they had been innocent farmers, somehow picked on and unilaterally attacked by us, were laughable. The fact that the inquiry was running with this idea, that this suggestion was even half taken seriously, felt disrespectful to everything we'd done that day. If those lawyers had been in the middle of what we'd been in the middle of, the sheer wildness of that engagement, they wouldn't have been stood there, asking me these questions. We were the British Army. We were trained, professional soldiers. We didn't just drive down the road to randomly pick a fight with some civilian farmers for shits and giggles. We'd been ambushed by militia and we'd been lucky to have come out alive.

'One of the two men that may have been detained by you and Mr Falconer, Abbas Al-Hameedawi – subsequently given the detainee number 776 – describes being approached by three soldiers, one of whom was black, that his hands were cuffed tightly, he was then pushed to the ground and kicked in the head by the black soldier. Did you see that?'

Beer had a long list of accusations about what had supposedly happened after the battle. Another detainee claimed he'd been kicked in the back and had fallen on his face, had been hit on the temple with a rifle butt, had been beaten and dragged into a personnel carrier. None of them directly related to me, did you see this? did you see that? It all felt a bit sneaky. No doubt they were asking the other soldiers if they'd seen me do stuff, trying to get each of us to snitch the others in. The odd thing about the questioning was that Beer then asked me about Lance Corporal Muir, who gave medical aid to two Iraqis and performed CPR on one of them. For all Beer's accusations to be correct, it would mean we would have been both beating up and treating the Iraqi soldiers simultaneously. Which just didn't make any sense at all.

'You were subsequently given an order that all the dead were to be collected,' Beer asked. 'Was an explanation given for the order?'

'I just remember it being passed down,' I replied. 'It was a pretty random order, I thought at the time, because we've never done that before. Normally the way it happens is once there's an engagement like that, a battle like that, then enemy is normally left in situ. So I did raise an eyebrow.'

Beer seemed suspicious over this decision, but there was a sound military reason behind it. Brigade thought that the militia leader might have been among the enemy dead or POWs, so they wanted everything brought back to camp to check. It was a brutal thing to have to do and was one of the parts of that day that affected me a lot later on. There were guts all over the place, arms hanging off, gunshot wounds to the shoulders. One of the other soldiers, I remember, couldn't handle it and was violently sick. At the end of the day, these were young men we were carrying. I know that they were enemy forces, but they were just people. And we were professional soldiers, yes, but we were people too. It was a difficult order to carry out – mentally, physically, emotionally. It's an experience that has stayed with me, with all of us who had to do that. If only the lawyers could have understood how we'd felt about that they'd have known immediately that the accusations levelled against us couldn't have been true.

Beer kept asking me questions about it, but it was a difficult subject to talk about and I struggled to keep my emotions out of my answers: 'I just remember by that time no one wants to do that and you were just getting told to put bodies in the back – I can't remember Warriors moving in and around any sort of area, but having to do that, I wouldn't wish it on anyone.'

I was doing something which would have tested anyone. I'd done it by switching off and just doing it and trying not to think about it. So although Beer was asking me question after question about what I could remember, which body went in which vehicle, I simply couldn't recall. Eventually, he got the point and moved on.

'Was there an incident where one of the detainees made a request for water?' Beer was now focusing on the journey back to camp from Danny Boy. He quoted my statement, where I said, 'During the journey none of the detainees were provided with food or water as we did not have any on the Warrior and it was only a short drive back to CAN.'

'Yes,' I said.

'Was he doing this by puckering his lips up as if he wanted water?'

'Yes.'

'But he wasn't provided with water; is that right?'

'No.'

'Why was that?'

'Because I think there was only one bottle left.'

'Who had that then?'

'Us in the back.'

Beer compared this account to my statement. 'Is it in fact the case that you did have some, but you had it rather than them?'

'I think if there was any water left, then we would have had it so there wouldn't have been any left.'

So much detail about a bottle of water, I thought. They were trying to make something out of nothing. We had a very short supply of water, water that was hot because of the temperature we were in. It wasn't that far back to camp, the detainee would survive without a drop of water. He hadn't been carrying bodies around. He hadn't been carrying 35 pounds of kit and a weapon. He'd just been trying to kill me and now he wants me to give him a drink of water. Tough.

'Did you have anything to do with the dealings with the detainees when you arrived at Camp Abu Naji?' Beer asked.

Finally, I thought. I could feel a bit of relief rushing through me, because I knew we'd reached the end of Beer's questioning.

'I remember arriving back at Camp Abu Naji and there was so much going on,' I replied. 'As soon as the door come open, it was quite bright because there were lights, spotlights, in the front of Camp Abu Naji. I remember getting out, stepping out of the vehicle, speaking with the RSM, which I think was RSM Whyke at the time, and then him taking control of the detainees from there.'

The detainees had become someone else's problem at that point. And Beer was going to become their problem now as well. He was done with me. I'd got through. I felt a mixture of things at this point: relieved, yes, drained, yes, but above all, pissed off. Pissed off with the way that every single thing we'd done on the battlefield had been scrutinised and challenged. That sense that I was to blame. We were to blame for having done our job.

'Thank you very much,' Beer said. 'If you wait there, there will be some questions from some other people,' he added blandly.

I took a sip of water and waited for round two.

CHAPTER NINETEEN

ROUND TWO

'**COLOUR SERGEANT WOOD,** my name is Steven Powles and I ask questions on behalf of the Iraqi core participants.'

As soon as Powles stood up, I didn't like him. I know you shouldn't judge a book by its cover, but as I said earlier, he had an attitude to him. While Beer had been coming to the task neutrally, Powles had interests he was defending. Rather than following the events through like Beer had done, he cut straight to the points he wanted to talk about.

There were no niceties. He immediately pulled up part of my statement about the 'standard operating procedure of disarming, disorientating and maintaining the shock of capture'.

'How were you trained to disorientate detainees?' he asked.

'Blindfolds or goggles blacked out with black masking tape.'

'What would be the purpose of disorientating them?'

Powles's questions seemed laced with suspicion. But I answered as best I could. 'Just to make sure that, one, they are not seeing what we have got in our vehicles because some of the kit in there is secret; two, when they get back to Camp Abu Naji, that they don't see key places, such as the ops room, where the loading bay is, stuff like that. So if they are brought back, they don't see the key sort of stuff that we have within our FOBs.'

'What do you understand by "the shock of capture"?'

'Just separating them. So they are going to be shocked because one minute they are fighting together, then next minute they are on their own. So that's going to be a shock to them. That would be a shock to anyone.'

'Yes,' Powles came back, 'and an unpleasant experience.'

'If you say so.'

Powles's attitude seeped through his comments. He seemed to me to have the starting point that we were in the wrong and his clients were in the right.

'Were you aware that the detainees you had were likely to be interrogated upon their return to Camp Abu Naji?'

'I was a junior commander. I had not even done any sort of battle course so I couldn't possibly comment on any interrogation.'

'Was one of the purposes of maintaining the shock of capture to keep the detainees in a disorientated state at the time that they were to be interrogated or TQ'd [tactically questioned]?'

'I'm not a trained practitioner on TQ'ing so I wouldn't know. The private soldier to lance corporal is taught the basics on that, and that is just, as I have told you then, try to keep them separated. I didn't know about the whole side of interrogation or TQ'ing, so ...'

'At paragraph 16 of your Inquiry witness statement,' Powles interrupted me. He obviously hadn't got what he wanted, so moved straight on. It felt like he was trying to keep me on my toes, wrong-foot me. 'You deal with searching for items and anything found on an individual being kept in a clear plastic bag. Do you remember that? What was the purpose of keeping items in a clear plastic bag?'

'Just so they don't get contaminated with our sort of fingerprints and stuff like that.'

'Was any effort made to identify which plastic bag contained items belonging to an individual detainee?'

'Not as I saw.' It hadn't been my job to do that. Someone else had been involved in sorting all that out.

'Were you given any training in terms of identifying whether particular weapons that you had obtained had come from a particular detainee?'

'It's an enemy weapons system. So the training that we were given was to unload that weapons system and then put it to the side because that will then be used in evidence.'

'If it was to be used in evidence, was any effort made to link any particular weapon with a particular detainee?'

Was any effort ... was any effort ... The way Powles phrased it, it made us sound as though we couldn't be bothered, weren't doing our jobs properly. But his questioning was completely the wrong way round. In the sort of situation we were facing, your sole priority is to get all the weapons systems, unload them and make them safe. You don't start making a list of which rifle belongs to which detainee.

'You say that you don't know if anyone fixed bayonets on 14 May 2004,' Powles swung the questions round again. 'You are quoted in two separate interviews as describing individuals with bayonets. Do you remember doing that? Telling journalists that you had seen people with bayonets fixed?'

'Not seeing people with bayonets fixed,' I corrected. 'Hearing that bayonets were fixed. I don't think I was quoted saying that I had seen people with bayonets fixed and, if I was, then that is just taken out of context.'

'You say you can't say if Corporal Byles fixed his bayonet. Are you trying to distance yourself from what you may have seen him doing with his bayonet?'

'No,' I dead-batted his accusation back. 'Because bayonets should have been fixed.'

The question moved on to the detainees we'd apprehended in the first trench. 'You say one was shouting and animated. You say he didn't have a weapon at the time that you saw him; is that right?'

'No, the weapon was on the floor, yes.'

'You didn't see him with a weapon?'

'He was never stood up with a weapon, no.'

'He was obviously speaking in Arabic or Iraqi,' Powles said. 'Could you understand what he was saying? Is it possible that he was protesting his innocence, that he had nothing to do with all of this?'

'No,' I replied. This is ridiculous, I thought. To suggest that the Iraqis we'd captured were unarmed and innocent would have been laughable if it wasn't so serious.

Powles asked me whether I'd reinforced my commands 'with any use of physical force or violence'.

I shook my head. 'It was a case of putting my arm on his shoulder once an engagement had happened and going into some sort of cover because, me, I was vulnerable and I didn't want to become a casualty and I don't think he would have wanted to be a casualty either.'

That seemed a reasonable point to me. Powles ignored it. Instead, he quoted back a line from my August 2004 statement where I said, 'four enemy stood, put their hands in the air and surrendered.' He asked about Corporal Byles and what he was doing at this point: 'I just know what I did and Rushforth did,' I told him. 'I can't account for his accounts unless I did visually see them, but I didn't because there was that much going on.'

'You didn't visually see him dealing with the four detainees that you and Rushforth dealt with?'

Visually see? 'No,' I confirmed.

'You say that you were the first into the position with Rushforth.'

'Yes,' I agreed, wondering where he was going with this.

'If that's right, you must have either yourself hit or kicked those detainees or seen either Corporal Byles or Tatawaqa kick or hit those detainees.'

That wound me up. Powles wasn't just suggesting that I or one of my colleagues had hit or kicked the detainees, the way he phrased it was taking that as a given. Someone had hit or kicked them, so was it you or someone else? I couldn't work out how he'd come to that conclusion, or how that followed from the questions he'd just asked.

'How?' I asked.

Powles didn't explain but came back again. 'Did you see anyone hit or kick any of the detainees?'

'No,' I said. I had a lot of eye contact with Powles during these exchanges. A good straight eyeball, to say no, I'm not afraid of you. I didn't like his questioning, or the way he was going about it. It seemed deliberately designed to try and trip me up, slipping in accusations as facts to see if I'd confirm them. Then, when he didn't get the bite he wanted, he'd change tack on to something else.

'You also say that one of the detainees had flip-flops,' Powles said. 'Do you know what happened to his flip-flops?'

Seriously? I thought. Flip-flops? That was the last thing I was worried about. He grilled me about the time spent with the detainees. 'Were you doing anything to maintain the shock of capture?' Again, I wasn't really sure what he was driving at. 'Were you shouting at the detainees?' Powles asked.

'No ... they were just doing what they were told by that stage,' I said. As if there was some sort of premeditated plan for keeping the prisoners confused, if that was what he was getting at. It just didn't work like that.

'Was there any need to stick a weapon in the back of one of those detainees when he was face down, lying down, doing what he was told?'

It was another one of those questions where there was a given in there about what we'd done. Powles was referring to a photograph taken, which I think showed Byles in that position. But I hadn't been there at the time the picture was taken, so I couldn't really comment, as much as Powles wanted me to. But if Byles had done that, there would have a been a reason for doing so.

'I wasn't there all the time so I don't know. I can't account for anyone else. I don't know if he tried to stand up, tried to move. If that's the escalation of force, to make sure that in that militia soldier is to lie down, then it is the escalation of force. I don't know. I wasn't there. I can't remember a weapons system. But clearly it has happened because there's a picture, but I wasn't there at that point or I can't remember.'

'Would it be appropriate to have your photograph taken with a detainee?' Powles changed the subject again.

'What, like that one?'

'Well, not necessarily that one. The one that you are in or the two that you are in.'

'I don't think it is appropriate,' I agreed, 'but it's happened.'

'Were they trophy photographs?'

'I don't think they were because I only seen them for the first time on Friday. So if they were that much of a trophy, I would have seen them before now.'

Powles switched back to Falconer and me clearing the other two positions. He quoted my inquiry witness statement, where I said, 'My memory as to the next sequence of events is very vague now as I seem to recall that everything happened at once.'

'You also say that you don't remember six people being killed, but can only remember two people being killed in the sequence of events thereafter.'

'Yes.'

'Is the reality that you don't want to tell this Inquiry as to the circumstances as to the other four people being killed and how they died?'

Wow, I thought. You've got some nerve, throwing these accusations about, questioning who I am. I eyeballed Powles. 'No, not at all.'

'In relation to the two detainees that surrendered to you, you are absolutely clear, aren't you, that neither of them were armed.'

I really didn't like how he was putting words into my mouth. 'I physically didn't see them with weapons systems or can't remember,' I corrected.

'Is it right that when you were walking one of them or escorting him, that he stumbled?'

Powles knew full well I did, quoting my August 2004 statement, where I said, 'Male 5 kept stumbling and one of his leather sandals which was a flip-flop design kept falling off.'

Of course, Powles had a suggestion for why this man was stumbling: 'Did you hit that man with a rifle butt?'

'No,' I snapped, 'but I'll tell you what did happen is the sergeant major picked his flip-flop up and threw it to the side because we were still massively vulnerable, bearing in mind we had been in a massive firefight for a couple of hours and we needed to get off the battlefield quickly and it was his flip-flop was on, his flip-flop was off, on, off, on and he warned him next time – clearly if he didn't speak English, didn't understand English, he didn't know what was going on – so he grabbed his flip-flop and threw it to the left-hand side.'

That accusation riled me. This guy had been messing about. We didn't know if he was deliberately trying to slow us down, playing games with us. Certainly, he was smirking away, so the sergeant major said, 'Right,' threw it to the side and said, 'Now fucking walk.' As I said, we were vulnerable and wanted to get off the battlefield. Why would we hit him with a rifle butt? That would only slow us down, create another drama when we really didn't need one.

Powles asked me about the loading of the bodies and then about the journey back to camp. 'Now, in relation to the journey back to Camp Abu Naji in the Warrior, you say that there was an Iraqi detainee who was puckering his lips indicating he wanted water for 15 to 20 minutes ... so is it right even though, according to you, there was water on the back of the Warrior, you left this man without water for some 15 to 20 minutes?'

'Yes, because we had one bottle which was for us, bearing in mind we had been on the battlefield for five hours and we were pretty dehydrated.'

'So was denying him water part of maintaining the shock of capture?'

Again, the conspiracy. 'Not at all. It was looking after us first.'

'You say at one point that the vehicle was plunged into darkness. At that point, did either you or anyone else hit him?'

'No,' I said. He kept the empty accusations up right until the end, I'd give him that.

We were all but done. Powles had one last piece of conspiracy to throw at me. 'Were you aware of an order by Major Coote on 21 May 2004 that no one was to talk to the Royal Military Police without first being briefed by him and that they should have an officer or a senior non-com-missioned officer present at the time?'

I wasn't and there wasn't. Powles asked about when I spoke to the RMP at Camp Abu Naji. 'Did you do so with an officer?'

'I can't remember.' And I couldn't. Because that tour was so intense, because we were in and out of action and car-nage, I couldn't recall because the process had been so quick and skimpy. Powles, I could tell, didn't believe me.

'Have you spoken to the RMP on many occasions during your army career ... the only two occasions upon which you spoke to the RMP were May 2004 and August 2004?'

'Yes,' I agreed, 'that is probably my first times, really, of speaking to the Royal Military Police.'

'And you can't remember it?' Powles sounded incredulous.

'No.'

'And you can't remember who was with you?'

'No.'

'Thank you very much.' Powles turned away and looked at the chairman. 'Those are my questions, Sir.'

Powles sat down, his final implication clear. The state-ments I'd given were somehow cooked up and my accounts of what happened weren't to be believed. My mind was all over the place. I felt tired and frustrated, but angry too. He'd been allowed to stand up and make all kinds of accu-sations against me with complete impunity, call me a liar, a murderer and everything in between. He, like Beer, was someone who had not been in the situations I had. Powles, as far as I was concerned, had no credibility to ask me those questions. When I came back on his accusations, he didn't back them up, just moved on to the next one. I felt pretty isolated sat up in that dock – ridiculed as the rest of the room looked on and listened to me try to defend myself.

The remainder of the session was taken up with questions from Melanie Cumberland and Neil Sheldon. Compared to the questioning I'd had already, the time I spent with them was comparatively short, but at least these later discussions felt more balanced.

'I ask questions for the Ministry of Defence,' Cumberland began. 'You said this morning that although this area was hostile during the time you were there in 2004 and you were engaged, as you said, near enough twice each day, that the engagement on 14 May was different because you had been ambushed, you had to come to a halt and you had been given a command to dismount. Would it also be right to say that on the other occasions when you had come under contact, the attacks had been less organised, the enemy were fewer and less challenging to suppress or avoid?'

Although I'd had no contact with the MoD prior to my appearance, from that opening question I could tell that she was much more on my side than the previous lawyers.

Her opening question was more along the lines I'd been expecting, putting the events of Danny Boy into context and trying to give the chairman and others in the room a bit more sense of precisely what it was I'd been through. I could feel myself relaxing a little and my answers became longer as a result.

Cumberland's starting point on Danny Boy was the opposite to Steven Powles's. 'You said that you consider that it was a pre-planned ambush. What made you think that?' she asked. 'It also involved, did it not a significant number of enemy gunman? And those enemy gunman were heavily armed?' Cumberland went on to list some of the weapons that we'd seized, which neither Beer nor Powles had mentioned: 'Two armed RPG launchers with grenades, two empty RPG launchers, belts of ammunition, five or six AK47 rifles and a machine gun.'

Compared to the previous questions, it was a bit like being bowled at underarm: 'Yes ... that is correct, yes ... totally, yes' were my answers.

Cumberland went to tackle the suggestions from Beer and particularly Powles head on. 'A number of the detainees captured on 14 May have said they were not involved in an ambush mounted with the intention of killing British troops, but rather were involved in innocent farming activities on that day in the area. You have already said that the four detainees that you dealt with in trench 1 were found in the presence of significant quantities of weapons.' She paused. 'Did you see on or near the detainees any farming implements, such as spades or sickles, which might suggest that what the detainees say they were doing in the area is true?'

In a way, the question was as ridiculous as some of the questions Steven Powles had asked. It seemed crazy that I had to answer it, but was glad that I had the opportunity to do so.

'No,' I replied. 'One of them photos – I don't know what photo it was – but that was, you know, pretty much how it was synced: weapon systems out, ammunition out for quick reloading. The belts were out. So unless they use that for farming tools ...' I paused, tried to keep a straight face. 'There was no picks or shovels or any indication that they were farmers. No tractors or anything like that, or cattle. It was just them and their weapon systems and ammunition.'

That was all Melanie Cumberland asked. Neil Sheldon, my own lawyer, was even more brief. He picked up on a couple of my answers regarding the gathering of weaponry and the possibility of identifying which weapon had belonged to which detainee. He got me to clarify those and that was it.

'Colour Sergeant,' the chairman turned to me. 'That completes your evidence to the Inquiry. Thank you very much for having come here in order to give your evidence to me. I am very grateful to you for that. I am also very grateful to you for your patience and courtesy in the way you have listened to and answered the questions which you have been asked in the way that you have done. Thank you very much indeed. You are now free to go and I wish you well for the future.'

By the time I stood down and was taken back to the holding room, I was exhausted. It had been hours of questioning, being made to relive things I didn't want to relive, and I felt drained. I could feel my head throbbing from the intensity of it all.

My lawyer, Neil Sheldon, seemed pleased. He echoed what the chairman had said, told me that I had handled myself with great dignity and that I'd presented myself well. I got my stuff together and I made to go. As I was leaving, funnily enough, I saw Tatawaqa coming in, who was going to be interviewed that afternoon. It was strange seeing him there. We nodded at each other and then I was on my way to catch the Underground.

I took the train back to Lucy's parents and stayed there until the Wednesday, when I hired a car to drive to Birmingham, took a trooper flight to Hannover, then a bus back to camp. It was good to be back in familiar surroundings and to see Lucy. I didn't really chat about the inquiry appearance with anyone, I hadn't spoken to her parents about it when I'd been staying there, or mine for that matter. Lucy asked me how it went and I said, 'The best it could go really.' I didn't really speak to her about it in any huge detail. I didn't want her to worry.

The conversations with the regiment about it weren't any more thorough. I was called up by the adjutant at the time, Captain Burgess, and he asked me how it went. 'Are you all right?' 'I'm fine,' I said. 'Okay, well just keep me posted.' And that was that, really. From the legal team, I didn't hear much more. I was told I'd be notified on where things would go next, but essentially, it was now a waiting game. Waiting for all the evidence to be collected, the remaining witnesses to be interviewed and the inquiry to pass its judgement on what happened that day in Iraq.

CHAPTER TWENTY

FALLOUT

I LEFT THE ARMY in 2014. That was a little bit because of the constant issues with Al-Sweady, but mainly because of what happened with my pension. Being a soldier had been what I was about, those values and standards and principles meant a lot to me. But I lost faith in the system. And once I lost faith, then I had to go.

The pension was the straw that broke the camel's back. Definitely. I did a lot of research into my position and wrote to the Armed Forces Pensions in Glasgow to get clarification. They confirmed what I'd feared. Because I'd had that gap year after 2006, it meant that my pension was different to all of my peers. They were going to get their gratuity lump sum after 22 years' service and then an immediate pension. I wasn't going to see anything until I was 65. I'd gone back in after that gap year assuming that I was going to continue on that pension. But it wasn't until they announced the changes to the pension scheme that I thought I should check things out. And I was in for a shock.

Glasgow told me I had to write a letter to the Military Pension Scheme, which I did, and they came back saying that I was not entitled to anything until I was 65 because of my break in service. My immediate response to that was,

Fucking hell, I am out of here. There was no incentive for me to stay now, even though I was a senior colour sergeant just about to pick up promotion to sergeant major. My CO and regiment went in to bat for me, spoke at length to brigade to see if anything could be done. But they couldn't shift them. So I went in to see the CO one morning. I marched into his office, saluted him, and he told me to stand at ease. He was gutted for me. Absolutely gutted for me because there was nothing that he could do. He didn't want to lose me but he did not have anything to persuade me to stay.

The promotion board is going to come up, the CO tried. *You are due to pick up company sergeant major, can you not think about it?* And I said, *What would you do?* He could not really answer that, because he would have done the same as me. He would have gone. There was no way I could have carried on. I would have been too angry and not put in the best I could do because I knew I was working without having the reward for the years I had put in. The good thing was, I had my house back in the UK. I had that as my sort of backup and I believed in myself that I would work it out. I would have done anything outside to start with – swept the street, whatever it took, to keep my family moving initially. But I had the self-belief that I'd find something worthwhile in time. And that is when I signed off.

I don't know how many people had similar pension problems. There was another from my regiment who was in the same situation. He spent two years out, got back in, then discovered the deal with the pension and left again. Which was another waste. I think they have changed the system now, so if you were in my position, your pension would carry on. But that came too late for me. I was gone.

It all seemed quite ironic. The reason that I'd got into this situation with my pension was because I'd taken that time out. And the reason that I'd taken that time out was, essentially, because of everything that happened in Iraq and how I'd struggled to deal with things afterwards. I'd taken the time out to get my head back together, but having done that, all that happened was that I got whacked over my pension as a result. That battle turned out to bite me on the arse in more ways than one.

I had been in the army for the long haul. I had visions of wanting to be a regimental sergeant major. That would have been the pinnacle of my career. And I was on course by a good shot to achieve WO1 (warrant officer class 1), as they call it. Even now, I do sometimes think about it. If I had stayed in, I would easily have been a company sergeant major by this point. Maybe even an RQMS (regimental quartermaster sergeant). But when I found out about the pension, it felt as though something was stopping me from progressing. That gap year was coming back to haunt me at the same time as Al-Sweady was going on. The lack of government support there combined with the rigidity over the pension felt like two sides of the same coin. For all I had done, there was a lack of support coming back.

It was a scary moment. What should have happened is that you left the army with a lump sum, to help you on that transition to Civvy Street. But because of my situation, I didn't get any of that. Because we'd been living in Germany, our UK house was being let out, so we had to serve notice on that. Then I started to think about what I might do.

I should have had what is called a dine-out. If you are in the Warrant Officers' and Sergeants' Mess, you have a regimental dinner with fellow mess members. But I didn't want any of that. With Al-Sweady and everything going on, I just wanted to slip out quietly. So I had some quiet drinks with a few close friends and that was it. In February 2014, four months after my appearance at the Al-Sweady Inquiry, we packed up, the removals guys came and we headed back to England.

I'd be lying if I said it wasn't an emotional moment. The army had been such a big part of my life – it was my adult life, all I'd known as an adult. And I'd loved it. I loved the belonging, I'd loved the purpose. It was going to be a challenge, for sure, adjusting to the real world and working out what it was I wanted to do.

Strangely enough, the first job I took in the real world saw me heading back to Iraq. I got a gig working for Control Risks on an ExxonMobil project, providing close protection for their American personnel. I was based in Erbil in northern Iraq and my job was to protect and transfer people between their hotels and the oil platforms for business meetings. It was all fairly routine stuff, but it paid well so was a good starting point to bank some cash.

Erbil was a completely different set-up to the Iraq I'd seen on my previous tours. The atmospherics were completely different. It was the capital of Iraqi Kurdistan and a lot more settled. Because of the oil in the region, it was beginning to get a lot of investment and had that up-and-coming feel. Maybe how Dubai felt a few decades earlier when that started to grow. I could go out in a way that I never could when on tour; then you never went beyond the wire. Here you could go out and eat in a restaurant. I'd go jogging in the park.

The protection we had was fairly minimal. On a job, we'd have an AK-47 with four or five magazines, which is nothing compared to the amount of kit I was used to. We'd have a set of three armoured wagons to go out in – vehicle front, vehicle middle, vehicle rear. So not a huge amount of support. My team was me and a couple of lads who used to be in the Parachute Regiment. We were all in a sort of similar place, using the skill set we had from the army and going on the circuit.

For me, it wasn't something that I wanted to do long term. It was a quick fix, to get some money in and help me get on my feet.

I was out there for nine weeks, during which time there was an announcement about the Al-Sweady Inquiry. It was weird to be in Iraq, reading about Al-Sweady on the Internet and trying to catch up with what was going on.

'We would like, with your permission, sir, to state our position on behalf of the Iraqi core participants on an important issue before this Inquiry.'

The first indication of how the findings of Al-Sweady might go came on the penultimate day of the hearings. It was 20 March 2014, just over four months after my questioning – and part way through my nine-week rotation at Exxon in Iraq – when Patrick O'Connor QC, one of the lawyers representing the Iraqis, asked for permission to address the inquiry.

'It is our duty,' O'Connor said, 'to assess the state of the evidence and only to advance submissions to you on a basis which we consider, in our professional judgement, to be properly arguable ... we feel that it is in the interests of all concerned and in the public interest to clarify our position in this important respect at this stage.' The position that O'Connor was referring to specifically were the accusations of unlawful killing against British soldiers. In a complete about-turn to the case his team had presented to the inquiry, O'Connor told the chairman that, 'The Iraqi core participants will not submit that, on the balance of probabilities, live Iraqis captured during the course of the battle on 14 May 2004 died or were killed at Camp Abu Naji.'

Public Interest Lawyers released a statement to reiterate this, saying: 'Following the conclusion of the military evidence and current state of disclosure by the MoD it is our view there is insufficient material to establish that Iraqi civilians were unlawfully killed whilst in the custody of British troops at Camp Abu Naji.'

It was an extraordinary intervention. The accusations of unlawful killing were the most serious charges levelled against British troops. Now, the lawyers representing the Iraqis were withdrawing the claim. It was an astonishing climbdown and one that threatened to undermine their whole case. If the most serious of the accusations against British forces weren't true, what did that mean for the rest of them?

Back in the inquiry, O'Connor said, 'The Inquiry has heard from a number of Iraqi witnesses, both detainees and other witnesses, about possible sightings or contact with some deceased whilst still alive, on the battlefield, in Warrior vehicles and at Camp Abu Naji. It is right to acknowledge that this evidence has been clarified and has significantly weakened during the Inquiry process.'

I'm not a lawyer, but over in Iraq even I could read between the lines of the legal speak to understand what O'Connor was suggesting. Once he'd finished making his statement, the chairman of the inquiry, Sir Thayne Forbes, spoke to thank and even praise him for his intervention. 'I do regard this statement as being one of very considerable significance and of great importance to the further progress of this Inquiry. I am extremely grateful for you having made this statement and for having done so at the time you have done it. I have absolutely no doubt that a great deal of anxious thought and consideration has gone into making the decision to make this statement and you and your team are to be commended for the courage that you have displayed in making this statement at the stage that you did. In my view, it is in the highest traditions of the English Bar.'

Forbes's basic decency in praising O'Connor shone through in his reaction to the statement. But in the highest traditions of the English Bar? Subsequent events and revelations would raise other questions. Certainly that wasn't the opinion of the solicitors representing the soldiers, who subsequently claimed that 'most of the evidence given by the Iraqi core participants to this Inquiry is now accepted by their own representatives to be unreliable.' The MoD team, meanwhile, said that, 'the entire factual basis upon which the judicial review claim was brought is untrue.'

A few weeks later, the various counsels to the inquiry gave their oral closing addresses. Patrick O'Connor spoke first, and at length, on behalf of the Iraqi participants. In legal speak, he tried to dismiss the claims against the Iraqi accusations as 'evidential disagreements between the core participants'. Of the criticisms from the soldiers' solicitors and those of the MoD, he said, 'They both dismiss all allegations of mistreatment at Camp Abu Naji ... They roundly condemn every Iraqi witness, save for one who is named, as either dishonest and unreliable. They commend every single military witness [as] honest and largely reliable, save of course for the very few who have broken ranks. This is a landscape which seems strangely tidy. It is an Arcadian fantasy.'

For O'Connor, the fact that the allegations of unlawful killings had been withdrawn was not something to be embarrassed about, but was 'an achievement of the Inquiry'. He said, 'the other core participants seek to found a generalised attack upon the good faith of the allegations of unlawful killings. The suggestion is that our concession made four weeks ago necessarily involves a concession of bad faith in the allegations being made. This is demonstrably untrue.'

This concession, as O'Connor described it, was not the only point that he was firefighting on. Another was over a document in Arabic entitled 'List of Detainees' Names for the British Occupying Forces'. This was an extraordinary document that purported to list the various detainees and which brigades of the militia each of them belonged to. It was clear evidence that the people we'd been fighting were anything but the innocent farmworkers they claimed to be. Yet as Neil Garnham QC, speaking on behalf of the soldiers' solicitors, said in his closing statement, the document 'came to be disclosed during the course of oral hearings and after all of the detainees had given evidence.' Garnham referred to a letter from Phil Shiner in late October 2013, just a week or so before I gave evidence: 'He said if this document, along with the other two disclosed to the Inquiry on 27 September 2013, had been brought to the attention of the Legal Services Commission, legal aid to bring the proceedings that resulted in this Inquiry would probably almost certainly not have been granted.' (Note however that the Chair of the Inquiry stated that the Arabic document in question did not bear directly on the central areas of inquiry and that it was primarily relevant to the credibility of key Iraqi witnesses.)

This document, it transpired, had been in the hands of legal firm Leigh Day for six years before being disclosed, though they had not been aware of its significance until much later. Stating the document 'should have been disclosed long ago', O'Connor said, 'It was a single sheet of paper lying, since 2007, somewhere in the files of solicitors who are not acting in this Inquiry and do not instruct us.' He tried to dismiss the document. 'It is only by a rather tenuous set of assumptions that the content has any relevance to any evidence before this Inquiry at all.' He claimed 'there is a complete lack of clarity as to the authorship and origin of this document.'

In his closing statement, Neil Garnham completely disagreed: 'on its face, the document would appear to confirm that the detainees were members of or associated with the armed insurgency. No credible explanation has yet been advanced as to why this document should be treated as anything other than face value.'

'The absurdity of much of the evidence given by the detainees,' Garnham continued, 'as to how they came to be on the battlefield should not obscure its significance in the assessment of their evidence as a whole. If the Inquiry concludes, contrary to their accounts, they were involved in the ambush, then they have all repeatedly, persistently and deliberately given false evidence, including on oath.'

This was a point backed up by the MoD's lawyer, Mr Johnson, who was the last of the three counsels to speak. 'We submit that the explanations given for the presence of the Iraqis on the battlefield is so incredible and so riddled with inconsistencies that it can very safely be rejected in its entirety,' he said. 'It is inconceivable,' he continued, 'that the accounts are based on honest mistakes independently made by different witnesses. The only reasonable inference is either that they put their heads together to concoct these false accounts, or that there has been some overarching directing force orchestrating the accounts they have given.'

The MoD weren't just critical of the Iraqi detainees in their closing statements, but also those who represented them. 'A great success of your Inquiry,' Johnson told the chairman, 'achieved necessarily at enormous public cost is ... to disprove the allegations of murder and torture that have so unfairly been made against courageous British servicemen.

Those allegations were given the veneer of respectability and the oxygen of publicity by their solicitor representatives.'

Speaking of which, despite all the evidence to the contrary, Patrick O'Connor maintained their legal take on the army's action right until the end. 'Sir,' he said, concluding his closing statement, 'it would indeed be a tidy landscape if our armed forces were safe from accountability to the rule of law. Some may describe that as Arcadian. Some others may describe it perhaps as Orwellian. Sir, we are witnessing the cold arrogance of the British state at work.'

It was now down to Sir Thayne Forbes to go off, sift his way through the mountain of evidence he'd been presented with and decide which of these deeply contrasting versions of events he agreed with.

Sir Thayne Forbes's final report on the Al-Sweady Inquiry was released on 17 December 2014, a year and a month after I'd given evidence. He'd certainly had a lot of material to work through: 169 days of hearings, evidence from 55 Iraqi witnesses, 222 service personnel and 4 expert witnesses; and a further chunk of written statements from another 328 witnesses. The final report he produced ran to over 1,200 pages and was so large it had to be printed in two separate volumes.

I don't know if leaving the army affected how much I knew in advance, but I didn't see anything prior to it being published. I did know from someone, I can't remember who, that the report summary and findings were coming out, and I was desperate to know what Forbes's conclusions were. I was at home on the day the documents were released and remember reading them on my laptop, poring over them at our dining-room table. I went straight to the executive summary – that was long enough in itself. I read that and the sections I'd been involved in, to discover what conclusions he'd come up with.

'At various stages during this report,' I started to read Forbes's conclusion with a sinking feeling, 'I have come to the conclusion that the conduct of various military soldiers and some of the procedures being followed by the British military in 2004 fell below the high standards normally to be expected of the British Army. In addition, on a number of other occasions, my findings went further. Thus as I make clear at various stages of this Report, I have come to the conclusion that certain aspects of the way in which the nine Iraqi detainees, with whom this Inquiry is primarily concerned, were treated by the British military, during the time they were in British custody during 2004, amounted to actual or possible ill-treatment.'

Reading that, it was difficult not to feel deflated. It felt measured and thoughtful, as I'd expected, but also seemed to give credence to the claims made by the Iraqi participants.

'However,' Forbes wrote on, 'I believe that it is very important to put these adverse findings about the British military and some of its individual soldiers into their proper perspective, by viewing them in the context of the original allegation which the Inquiry was asked to consider.'

I started to read on quicker. 'I have come to the firm conclusion,' Forbes wrote, 'that the vast majority of the allegations made against the British military, which this Inquiry was required to investigate (including, without exception, all the most serious allegations) were wholly and entirely without merit or foundation.'

Without merit or foundation. Wow. I had to read that twice, pinch myself to make sure I'd read it right.

Forbes was as strong in his criticisms of the Iraqi participants as he was in his conclusions: 'Very many of those baseless allegations were the product of deliberate and calculated lies on the part of those who made them and who then gave evidence to this Inquiry in order to support and perpetuate them. Other false allegations were the result of inappropriate and reckless speculation on the part of witnesses.'

That, though, was just for starters. 'I have also come to the firm conclusion that the approach of the detainees and that of a number of the other Iraqi witnesses, to the giving of their evidence, was both unprincipled in the extreme and wholly without regard for the truth. Such was the extent to which some of these witnesses told deliberate and calculated lies to this Inquiry, that I felt it necessary to indicate that such was the case.'

As damning as Forbes was on the Iraqi witnesses, he was also full of praise for the military ones. 'In contrast and except where otherwise expressly stated, for the most part I was generally impressed by the way in which the military witnesses approached the giving of their evidence,' he wrote. 'Some of them evidently found the process of giving evidence, including the need to recall the events with which this Inquiry was concerned, very difficult and distressing. Except where otherwise expressly stated, in general I found the military witnesses to be both truthful and reliable. For the most part, they used their best endeavours to recall details of events that had occurred nearly a decade previously.' He had thoughts, too, on the British military and the Battle of Danny Boy itself. 'Although my terms of reference do not permit me to investigate or comment upon the legality of the conduct of the British soldiers during the resulting battle, it does seem to me that the evidence clearly showed that the British soldiers responded to this deadly ambush with exemplary courage, resolution and professionalism.'

Forbes's conclusion couldn't have been clearer: 'The work of this Inquiry has established beyond doubt that all the most serious allegations, made against the British soldiers involved in the Battle of Danny Boy and its aftermath and which have been hanging over these soldiers for the last ten years, have been found to be wholly without foundation and entirely the product of deliberate lies, reckless speculation and ingrained hostility.'

For the accusations to have been withdrawn and refuted as comprehensively as this, it was an amazing feeling. I cannot describe what it was like to feel that weight lifting off my shoulders. It was immense. I wasn't sure what I was expecting to happen that day. If the findings had gone the other way, who knows what might have happened next. So for the inquiry to come up with these conclusions, to back up everything I'd said, it felt liberating, a release.

The inquiry did uphold some of the more minor claims of mistreatment. It suggested the detainees should have been given proper food and drink when they were first detained. That was a little dig at me. I could have given them water in the back of the Warrior and maybe I should have done. But as I said in my evidence, that wasn't part of some masterplan, but because we had a limited amount left and I thought we deserved it more. Being older now, I can look back and see that I should have given them some water. But compared to the larger accusations, criticisms like that or the tightness of the plasticuffs were relatively minor.

I felt bad, in a strange way, that so much money out of the public purse had been spent on the inquiry. I know it was out of my control and I wasn't to blame, but I still felt sorry because that money – £31 million – could have been spent in a more useful and appropriate way. But above all, I felt relief that the truth was out there and the soap opera of emotions I'd been through over those years was finally coming to an end.

I got a lot of calls from the press. Partly, I think, because I'd done a couple of interviews before, but also because I was one of the men who'd won the Military Cross in that battle. And I suspect, too, that it was easier to talk to me because I was no longer in the army – the media could contact me directly, in that regard. One of the newspapers I remember speaking to was the *Daily Mail*, who asked me what I thought of the findings. 'We have been dragged through five years of hell,' I told them. 'That in my view is a betrayal of our service. We did what we had to do as soldiers and we did the right thing.' It was a busy day, by the end of it my phone was red hot, with journalists ringing for quotes and mates texting to say what great news it was.

In the House of Commons, the secretary of state for defence at the time, Michael Fallon, gave a statement on the publication of the report. He began by quoting Phil Shiner from when he spoke at that original press conference in 2008. He contrasted those initial accusations with Forbes's finding in the report. He criticised the legal team of the Iraqi participants for withdrawing the accusations about unlawful killing so late in the proceedings. The delay, he said, was 'inexplicable and shameful'. He said expert witnesses had proved the previous July that the accusations couldn't have been true – 'had the concession been made then,' he noted, 'it would not have been necessary for so many soldiers to give evidence.' One of those soldiers, of course, being me.

Fallon was sharply critical of both the Iraqi witnesses and their legal team: 'The Iraqi detainees, their accomplices and their lawyers must bear the brunt of the criticism for the protracted nature and £31 million cost of this Inquiry.'

He revealed that the Solicitors Regulation Authority (SRA) had decided to investigate two firms – Phil Shiner's Public Interest Lawyers and Leigh Day, the firm that had the so-called 'militia list' – for breaches of professional standards. Had the Legal Services Commission been aware of the evidence that Leigh Day unwittingly had in their possession in 2008, he noted, there would have been no legal aid and no inquiry: 'that would have spared the service personnel a further six years of uncertainty and anxiety.'

'I regret that it was found necessary to hold a public inquiry to disprove these allegations,' Fallon told the House. 'This was not another Baha Mousa or an Abu Ghraib ... this was a shameful attempt to use our legal system to attack and falsely impugn our armed forces.' He again quoted Phil Shiner from the original press conference: '"Do not believe for one second," he said, "that we make these allegations lightly or without the evidence available to substantiate every single word of what we say."' Given the allegations had now been disproved, Fallon said, 'I challenge Mr Shiner and the other lawyers involved, from both firms, to issue an unequivocal apology to the soldiers whose reputations they attempted to traduce.'

Fallon saved one of his most powerful observations until the very end: 'I add only one final comment. Following the battle of Danny Boy, five soldiers were awarded the Military Cross and one the Conspicuous Gallantry Cross for their conduct there and in other engagements in early 2004.

Other acts of bravery emerge clearly in the accounts of the battle. This is who our servicemen and women are. The reputation of our armed forces has been hard won in the service of our nation. It will survive the baseless slurs of those who seek to undermine those on whom we all depend.'

It's unusual to get moved by something a politician says, but this was real lump-in-the-throat stuff. After being sat in that inquiry room, feeling isolated and hung out to dry by the MoD, it was good to finally hear them coming down on our side. And not only defending us, but acknowledging the bravery that we'd shown in that battle. After the long years of accusations, I'd be lying if I didn't say that felt good.

In fact, the only sour note that entire December day was the reaction of the lawyers involved. Fucking right, I thought, when Fallon said they owed the soldiers an apology. But PIL rejected that suggestion. When asked by the BBC on this point, John Dickinson, a PIL lawyer, said, 'I don't think it's for me to apologise for the situation which arose ... had the matter been dealt with far more speedily, and far cheaper, which it could have been, then this long delay would not have occurred ... to a large extent I think the MoD were responsible for this delay and for this cost.'

Speaking to the *Daily Mail*, he defended the inquiry, describing it as 'legally necessary, morally justified and politically required'. He denied that his legal team had lost: 'It would be a defeat if we were seeking to claim compensation, if we had been seeking to bring home a criminal conviction. The whole purpose of an inquiry is to inquire and we are content with the decisions and conclusions reached.'

That seemed unlikely to me. While Leigh Day were completely cleared of any wrongdoing by the Solicitor's Regulation Authority, in the months after the inquiry, PIL would have a lot less to be content about.

CHAPTER TWENTY-ONE

STRUCK OFF

THE FALLOUT FROM the Al-Sweady Inquiry was to continue for the next two years. Such were the sums of money involved in running the inquiry that it was felt necessary to explore quite how things had got to this point and what could be done in the wake of them.

The two firms who found themselves under the spotlight for their behaviour were Leigh Day and PIL. Leigh Day had not been directly involved in the inquiry itself, but represented the interests of the Iraqi participants in a civil lawsuit. It was they who had the 'militia list' document in their files, which confirmed that those detained were part of the local militia, rather than innocent farmworkers as they claimed. The firm had received the document back in 2007, on a trip to Syria. It was one page long, written in Arabic and its relevance was not appreciated at the time. There was also an original handwritten English translation of the document. The latter, for reasons that were unclear, was shredded but a copy had been typed up and retained by the firm. The firm later said, that whilst 'there was no dispute as to the accuracy of the translation, in retrospect we now recognise that the document should not have been thrown away.' The Arabic document remained on file with its significance not recognised; its existence, as we now know, was only revealed at a later stage in the inquiry after an order to disclose all relevant documents. (The Inquiry report stated: 'At this stage it suffices to say that the contents and nature of the OMS detainee list greatly reinforces and substantially confirms the conclusion that I have reached above, namely that each of the nine detainees participated actively in the ambush of, and attack, upon British troops that took place on 14 May 2004 and that it is very likely that each did so as a member of or volunteer in the Mahdi Army.')

Leigh Day, a respected legal firm, has a long history of successful cases. Leigh Day had been founded back in 1987 by the former Greenpeace chairman Martyn Day. Among its most high-profile successes had been getting compensation from the German and Japanese governments for prisoners of war and successfully suing the British government on behalf of a group of Kenyans for abuses committed during the colonial era.

PIL, who represented the Iraqi participants at the inquiry, had been founded by Phil Shiner in 1999 and he remained the sole director of the company. In 2004, he was named human rights lawyer of the year and in 2007 won the Law Society's solicitor of the year award. He, too, had previously taken on the government and won: over Gurkha prisoners of war and over the case of Baha Mousa, the Iraqi man who died while in British custody in 2003.

All of which made what happened in the Al-Sweady Inquiry all the more confusing. I don't think that Phil

Shiner was all dark by any stretch of the imagination. He was the gold standard of solicitors at the time when he made the accusations that would lead to the inquiry being launched. He had that credibility from having won those previous cases against the government, so when he said he had the evidence to back the claims up, people believed him. Quite where things went south, I don't really understand, but go south they did. And given what the inquiry put myself and the other soldiers needlessly through, my sympathy for his position was in somewhat short supply.

Following the release of the inquiry's report, the SRA began an inquiry into the conduct of PIL and Leigh Day. In June 2017, after a seven-week case, Leigh Day and three of its solicitors were cleared by the Solicitors Disciplinary Tribunal of all 19 charges of professional misconduct brought by the SRA, a finding which was confirmed by the Court of Appeal in 2018. In PIL's case, the outcome was somewhat different. In March 2015, the government turbocharged the process by sending the SRA its own dossier of evidence on the behaviour of PIL. The government's evidence made a number of claims but two were particularly shocking. Firstly, it suggested that PIL had misgivings over the credibility of the evidence of its clients in March 2013, but it was a full 12 months before it withdrew the allegations of unlawful killing.

Secondly, the dossier claimed that PIL had used a 'fixer' or agent in Iraq, who had made what it described as 'unsolicited approaches' to potential victims. The result of this deeply unethical process had been an explosion in the number of cases that PIL had filed against British forces – over 1,000 judicial review claims in total. The government announced its intention to sue PIL for millions of pounds and to push for Phil Shiner to be struck off as a solicitor.

As the investigation into Phil Shiner and PIL continued, in August 2016 it was announced that the Legal Aid Agency had decided that PIL had breached contractual require-ments and as such, it would no longer receive public funding. The upshot of that was that by the end of that month, PIL had closed down. It announced it would not act for 187 Iraqi claimants it was representing and would not bring for-ward a further 1,000 cases it had been intending to lodge.

Phil Shiner, meanwhile, was charged by the SRA on 24 counts. He tried and failed to have his disciplinary hearing held in private and in December 2016, it was announced that the case would be held in January 2017. Twenty-four charges were levelled against him, of which Shiner denied six, but he admitted to nine counts of acting without integ-rity and one of acting recklessly and partly accepted an additional nine. In a letter to the disciplinary tribunal, he admitted that he paid a fixer over £25,000 in referral fees to try and find clients, and that he had also doctored evi-dence in an attempt to cover his tracks. He also admitted to paying a witness to change their evidence regarding the identity of his clients in the Al-Sweady Inquiry.

When the hearing took place on 30 January, Shiner failed to appear, citing illness and stress. In his absence, the SRA counsel, Andrew Tabachnik, said, 'at the heart of Prof Shiner's misconduct [is his belief that] his work in the human rights field was of sufficient moment that he was entitled to ignore the rules that applied to fellow solicitors.'

Shiner attempted to tell the tribunal that because he was under a lot of stress he was not responsible for his actions and as a result his actions were not dishonest. But Tabachnik showed a trail of emails that dismissed this theory: 'The defence to the dishonesty aspect is effectively, "I was not in full control of my mental faculties at this time and I didn't know right from wrong and what I am doing." But what these emails establish is a pretty clear indication that … you're not dealing with someone incapable of working out whether he was behaving dishonestly or not.' Tabachnik also accused Shiner of 'manoeuvring' by attempting to change the remit of the tribunal and accused him of being in 'a state of avoidance' over what he had done.

The tribunal also heard a written statement from Colonel James Coote, who'd been in command at Danny Boy. 'The false allegations levelled against the soldiers in my command were among the most serious against the British army since the Second World War. I didn't think solicitors could simply make or endorse false statements. I recall my sense of anger and dismay about those allegations. The nature of those false allegations raised at a press conference resulted in an extremely stressful and demoralising decade for me and other soldiers.'

Four days later, the tribunal concluded, finding Shiner guilty of twenty-two misconduct charges, with the remaining two left on the file. He was struck off as a solicitor and ordered to pay the costs of the prosecution, beginning with a down payment of £250,000. IHAT (Iraq Historic Allegations Team) announced it would look again at the claims referred to it by Shiner and his team. Out of the 3,292 allegations that IHAT had received, almost two-thirds had come from Shiner's firm. The MoD, meanwhile, were keen to look at ways of recouping some of the millions that had been paid out to Shiner's firm. It claimed to have paid out over £100 million in legal costs and compensation linked to the Iraq War, out of which a significant amount was as a result of cases brought by PIL.

After the case Colonel Coote said that Shiner should now apologise. 'It would be appropriate if Shiner apologised now to the soldiers and their families for what they have been through,' he said.

So did the defence secretary, Michael Fallon: 'Phil Shiner made soldiers' lives a misery by pursuing false claims of torture and murder – now he should apologise.'

Phil Shiner did not apologise.

One month after being struck off, Phil Shiner declared himself bankrupt, ending any attempts by the MoD to recoup the money they felt owed.

One year later the Insolvency Service announced that it had discovered a series of financial deals that Shiner had struck before his bankruptcy. These included transferring his

£300,000 family home and even a couple of guitars that he owned into a family trust – the terms of the trust allowed him to continue living in the house. He then sold two properties for £550,000, transferring the money to PIL. He then took £170,000 out of the law firm, putting £95,000 into his pension and the rest into the family trust. The Insolvency Service extended his bankruptcy to six years for 'unacceptable behaviour', with Justin Dionne, the official receiver, saying, 'Mr Shiner thought he could be clever by giving away his assets to his family members so when he declared himself bankrupt there wasn't anything to pay his creditors with. Sadly he was mistaken as all his activities were easily spotted.' The Insolvency Service said it had recovered just under £500,000 but Shiner's outstanding debts remained at £6.5 million.

What happened with Phil Shiner, I guess only he really knows. His journey is a story in itself, from being lawyer of the year, to ending up struck off and bankrupt. Somewhere along the way, the moral compass that had been his guiding force went off. Whether he got blinkered, whether he got greedy, whether he believed his own hype, it's all speculation really. He must have known what he was doing was wrong. Using a middleman to come up with allegations, you just don't do that. He ended up going off course big time and paid the price for it.

But for all the sums of cash involved, he wasn't playing with money, but with people's lives. Rather than using his legal skills to look at the evidence rationally, he appeared to have got it into his head the idea that the British Army were bastards to a man and that he was going to bring them down. That was his starting point and he'd work the evidence and cut the corners until he'd got the case that he wanted to bring.

When Shiner was struck off, I was pleased. He could never now do again what he'd been doing and put people like me through the years of hell that he had dragged us through. Just as I'd lived through that experience for all those years, he was going to have to live with his lies for the rest of his life. It is justice in my eyes. If the case against him goes on and ends up in a criminal court, then he would deserve to face the consequences.

He never apologised. Even if he did now, I think it's too late. There was a time and a place to do so and he decided not to. I think he's heartless and a coward for not having done so. The contrast with the bravery shown by the troops at Danny Boy couldn't be sharper.

How should things have been done differently? Well, obviously the inquiry should never have happened in the first place. But when those initial accusations had been made, I think it should never have gone public. I think it could have been investigated thoroughly behind closed doors, to ascertain that there wasn't a case to be brought. Once it was out there, then all of us accused had our lives put at risk. You only need one extremist to track us down and think we were a legitimate target because of the alleged mistreatment. So I had years of locking my door three times, of doing my 5- and 20-metre checks before shutting the house up at night.

Having the accusations out there, and given credence by the public inquiry, it meant that it tarnished our names, tarnished the regiment, tarnished our achievements. Mud sticks. The fact that the government allowed that inquiry to happen makes me so angry. The fact that they did so, and then failed to offer us any support or backup, I still find staggering.

Some of those accusations, I can't believe that someone didn't smell a rat. One of the detainees claimed he had been out grazing cows on the battlefield when the action took place. Another claimed he'd been there because he'd been out buying 40 litres of yoghurt for a wedding. A guy without transportation making a 15-kilometre round trip to buy industrial quantities of yoghurt in the middle of nowhere. Where was the yoghurt? Did the cows eat it all? More seriously, someone should have looked at this stuff at the start and said, 'There's nothing to this. Let's move on.'

After Shiner was struck off, I was contacted by the media to give my reaction. I talked to various journalists and went on *Good Morning Britain*, though, sadly, not when Susanna Reid was on duty. It was after that, that I got an email from Major General Chalmers. He was the colonel of my regiment and since then had been promoted up through to major general. By 2017 he was working in America, as a liaison with the US Army. The email read:

Brian, as you may be aware I am half way through a two year tour with the United States Army and I am somewhat isolated from the UK. However, the news of Shiner's striking off and its impact on IHAT has found its way even as far as this part of Texas. I know that this has been a long twelve years for all those involved and the news is both significant and welcome, be it overdue ...

You have given up a considerable amount of your own time recently to explain to the public what you have all been through and the impact it has had on you, your family and others involved. Those that have seen, heard or read your interviews tell me that you maintained your dignity and composure despite the pressure and that you were a superb ambassador for the soldiers, the army and the regiment ... hopefully you may now be able to put the inquiry behind you all, allowing you and the others involved to get on with your lives.

I was so touched to get that email. Other people I'd served with, other high-ranking officers, the government and the MoD, I'd heard nothing from at all. But Chalmers had always been something of a legend, so to get that from him was very special. Compared to the lack of support I'd got from other quarters, this meant a lot.

CHAPTER TWENTY-TWO

STARTING OVER

AS THE INQUIRY and its aftermath continued to play out, I was attempting to get on with my life and forge myself a new career after leaving the army. That had started with the security job in Iraq and continued when I got offered a job to work for the regimental charity.

It had been during my nine-week rotation in Iraq that I got a call from Matt Maer. He said that they were looking for someone to front the Friends of PWRR, which is the regimental charity, which is there to help all serving and former serving personnel and their families. Matt asked if I'd be interested in becoming its head of fundraising as he thought I'd be good at the role. There was a guy called Nick Goble who co-founded friends of PWRR and he helped me out as a mentor, brought me in the day before the interview to run through some practice questions. When I got the job, he found some office space for me in a building in Clapham, which was really kind of him.

Matt was extremely supportive of me in that role. He explained to me that he thought it was a great stepping stone. Even if it wasn't what I wanted to do long term, it would be an invaluable experience and would really help in networking and meeting people. That would stand me in good stead for whatever I wanted to do going forwards. I was also incredibly fortunate to have the help of Sir Lloyd Dorfman. I went to see him and explained what it was I wanted to do and achieve and he said he would help out. I also spoke to Lisa Ryan, who is a close friend and a razor-sharp businesswoman. I learned massively from her. We discussed things we could do with the Friends of PWRR to take it forwards and how I could get the most out of the experience.

I got my brain in gear as to how we could raise money and came up with a series of events. One of these was to abseil off the top of the Spinnaker Tower in Portsmouth. I did it with Colonel Coote and Jay Baldwin, who was an above-the-knee double amputee. Jay is an incredibly brave guy and an all-round good bloke. He stood on an IED in 2012 and lost both of his legs above the knee.

I'm usually not bad when it comes to heights, but we got up to the top of the tower – it's 170 metres tall – and I was like, woah, the drop seemed huge. Because it was so high, there was a problem with the wind too. The first time we attempted it, the safety experts called it off because the winds were too strong. That sort of thing isn't great for your nerves. But eventually we did it and raised a lot of money in the process.

We arranged a big gala dinner at the Kingsway Hall Hotel, London, where we raised in excess of £70,000. We sorted out a summer cocktail fundraiser in the Tower of London, which was pretty cool, and another huge dinner there that raised touching on £60,000 as well. We did a 24-hour cycle in Canary Wharf, riding on fixed bikes while members of the regimental band played. That raised a lot of money.

But the biggest event we did was the Ride to Recovery, which was a cycle ride from one coast of America to the other. That was with Jay. Ever since he'd had his legs amputated, he'd had problems with the sockets that he'd got issued with. He had a lot of sores and phantom pains. One day he called me up to say that he'd heard about a pioneering new procedure called osseointegration. It was developed by a surgeon in Australia, Dr Munjed Al Muderis, and he thought it might solve his issues. Essentially the procedure involves fusing titanium implants into the injured limb. These implants then combine with adapters that work as the new joint, to which you attach the artificial leg.

For Jay, the surgery would be life-changing. But it came at a huge cost – including rehabilitation it totted up to around £100,000 in total. I spoke to Matt Maer about it and he said that we had to support Jay. The turnaround time was remarkable. Within a few weeks we were able to get the money signed off from the PWRR Benevolent Fund. We flew Jay to Australia for the treatment, along with a friend to accompany him. He had the surgery and then spent a month in rehab, where he learned to bear weight on the titanium rods and strengthen his rods. It changed his life completely. He can now walk, it's incredible.

When Jay got back to the UK, he rang me. He said that he wanted to do a charity event, something major that would raise a lot of money, which could then be put back in the Benevolent Fund in return for the money that had helped with treatment.

'That sounds like a plan,' I said to him. 'I'm in. So what do you want to do?'

'Wood-Pig,' he said, which was his nickname for me, 'Wood-Pig, I want to cycle across America.'

I laughed. 'What about the fact you haven't got any fucking legs?'

'No, you idiot. I mean hand-cycling.'

'You can't do that,' I said. 'Hand-cycle across America? Are you insane?'

But Jay, who was stubborn at the best of times, was not to be shifted. 'I'm going to do it. Let's start the planning.'

I spoke to Matt and the regiment and they agreed to support us. They gave us some manpower and we built up a team so we could attempt it. In total there were ten of us cycling, with a further group of support staff. One of the other cyclists was John Moore, who had served with the 1st Battalion for eight years and now lived in the States. He was brilliant and really helped us out. He drove over from San Diego to meet us in Washington DC, near where we were setting off.

We began at the nearby port of Annapolis, where we dipped our rear wheels into the water. The journey was around 3,000 miles in total and we were attempting to do it in 14 days. We'd decided to do it east to west, but having made our plans we learned that most people who attempted such a journey did it from west to east for one simple reason – headwinds. So if the challenge wasn't difficult enough, we were making it even more difficult for ourselves before we'd even started!

It was an unbelievable journey with some great people, but one not without its incidents and stresses. There was one point, I think it was just after we'd passed through Amish country, where we were cycling through this area which was all villages with houses and big front gardens and everyone seemed to have these enormous dogs. Because Jay was on a handbike, he was the most vulnerable, being the closest to the ground. So the rest of us agreed to cycle around him, in a group formation to box him in and protect him. Anyone who saw a dog on the loose would shout the direction – 'Dog Left!' 'Dog Right!' – and we'd go into this formation to protect him.

Most of the time, it was fine, because the dogs were usually chained up. But a few got out and tried to chase us. One time, I remember this brute of a dog coming out of nowhere, barking its head off. I shouted 'Dog Right!' and we all got in our positions to protect Jay. We pedalled hard and managed to run it off. I'd just shouted 'Clear!' when out of the corner of my eye I saw this other dog haring in. It was some sort of cross-breed, a bit German shepherd, a bit Rottweiler, and it flew past me into the middle of the bikes. Before we knew it, it had locked on to Jay and was biting him on the shoulder.

We were travelling at quite a pace at this point, because we'd been outrunning the previous dog. John Moore unclipped from his pedal and tried to kick the dog off. But as he did so, Jay pulled into him and the two collided and came off their bikes.

'Fucking hell!' Jay was shouting. 'Someone get this dog off me!'

In the melee I skidded and came off my bike as well. I picked up my bike and threw it at the dog. Finally, it released Jay. He had puncture wounds all over his shoulder and arm. 'That's it,' he said. 'Take me home. I've had enough of this now.' But we got him in the support wagon, took him to hospital where he had his jabs, got stitched up and 24 hours later he was ready to carry on again.

There were huge differences in the terrain. Working our way through Kansas I remember feeling a bit stir-crazy – a combination of the wind and the dead-straight roads that seemed to go on for days. In Arizona, the temperature was insane. The inner tubes were struggling in the heat and the support wagon had to go off to try and source some more. Meanwhile, we were running out of water and had to knock on strangers' doors because we were so thirsty.

But people were really generous. Not only did they give us water, I remember them stuffing our bottles with ice cubes to keep them cool. We got to Flagstaff where we met up with Mark Spicer, who was a former sniper instructor in the battalion and repatriation CSM for Christopher Rayment and Lee O'Callaghan. He'd arranged for some local press to do some interviews and after that we were getting people coming over and stopping us, giving us donations because they'd heard about us on the radio.

Eventually we got to Santa Monica, where the pier was our finish line. Matt Maer and his wife had flown out and they were there to greet us. We wheeled our bikes down the beach to the sea, and dipped our wheels in the water, just as we'd done at the start of the journey. It was an amazing achievement. I was so proud of everyone, but particularly of Jay for what he'd achieved. It showed to me the worth of what I was doing and how that hard work could really make a difference.

One of the events we had at the Tower of London included an auction. I managed to twist a few arms and arrange for one of the lots to be a weekend experience of spending time with one of the fighting units. This was the 2nd Battalion PWRR, who at this point were out in Cyprus. The winning bidder would fly out to Larnaca, where they'd be picked up by the battalion and taken to the Officers' Mess. They'd spend time in the Dismounted Close Combat Trainer, and then on the ranges where they'd experience firing British weapons under instruction. There'd be time spent with soldiers, a chat through everything from sniper stances to discussing kit and equipment – a first-hand experience of what being a soldier was really like. There'd be a full regimental dinner in the Officers' Mess and then time to explore Cyprus by quad bike. It was a fantastic package, really money-can't-buy-this-type stuff.

Sir Lloyd Dorfman was at the auction and when he asked me what I thought he should go for, I said the Cyprus experience like a shot.

'All right,' he said. 'I'm buying it.'

Lloyd is not someone used to coming second. So when the bidding started and another wealthy businessman started upping the offers, Lloyd came back. It was going up in price, from £6,000, to £7,000, to £8,000. Then Lloyd just said, '£14,000' and the room was so quiet you could hear a pin drop. Quiet until the auctioneer's hammer came down. Afterwards, Lloyd found me and said, 'I am going to take you on my plane. I want you to come with us.' By us, Lloyd meant Olly and Charlie, two guys running a business called The Office Group – a company that provides offices, meeting rooms and co-working spaces. There would also be a couple of people from Doddle, another upcoming organisation that Lloyd was involved in.

I drove up to Harrods Aviation at Luton Airport. It was like another world. There were people making a fuss of you, taking your luggage and all sorts. As I walked on to the plane, I took my shoes off, put them on a shoe rack as it was all cream carpets inside. Lloyd turned to me and said, 'Brian, you go in with the pilots. They will get the jump seat out and you can take the plane up.' I went up and it was incredible. They gave me a headset, so I could listen in to all the communications between the pilots and the tower. The flight was in the early hours of the morning, so I watched the sun come up. Amazing. I'd never been on a flight like it. I was used to bumping along in the back of a big bone-crusher of a transport plane, but here I was, being flown by private jet.

Over the weekend, I got to know Olly and Charlie. We hit it off really well and when we got back to London, they asked me to go and see them. We went out to a Nando's and had lunch and they told me about their plans for the business.

'We're growing,' Olly explained, 'and we need people to help us do that. If you're looking to move on, then you should come and speak to us, because we would rather have you than someone else.'

I went to see Nick Goble to talk about it, he said that it was an amazing opportunity and that I should go for it. So I did. I was nervous at first – this was my first proper job on Civvy Street, rather than one army related – but I soon found my feet and was able to use my skill set from being in the regiment. To begin with, I worked in the back end, on the operational side of the business. I realised that this was the same sort of logistics and distributional management stuff I'd done when I was a CQMS, so I plugged into those skills and got stuck in.

It does take time to adjust from the army to Civvy Street. I still feel I am adjusting even now. Organisation and structure is one of the differences. Being in the army, you're in an institution. For years I knew exactly where I needed to be and what time I needed to be there. I would always get myself to places ten minutes early. But in an office environment it's different – things overrun, people turn up late. I've had to learn to cut people a little slack and build a bit more flexibility into how I work.

Communication is another big difference. In the military, it is hardly ever done on email. You'd just go and see someone and speak to them face-to-face, to make sure they understood their role and responsibilities. Now you had people emailing you about something, even if they were just 10 metres away. Why don't you come and speak to me? I thought. Or pick up the phone and chat?

There are other differences too, small things, which I appreciate. Not having to shave every day. Wearing smart-casual clothes. And getting home to see Lucy and the kids, that's brilliant. I'm back in time to see them in the evenings, I'm there at weekends. I really enjoy having that part of family life. I would never go away again now. I couldn't imagine going off abroad for months at a time without seeing them, as I did on the military tours. Family, I've come to understand, is more important than anything.

In November 2017, I was working at one of The Office Group's buildings just off Oxford Street. At about 4.30pm in the afternoon, an altercation between two men at Oxford Circus Tube station led to mass panic and rumours of a terrorist attack. There were reports on social media of shots being fired, which then went on to be retweeted by various celebrities, which only raised the temperature still further.

It was chaos, people running everywhere. At the building I was working in, I quickly realised that I was the only person there with any experience of dealing with that sort of situation. Instinctively, the old army training kicked in. I was trying to get the building into lockdown, told people to get inside, find themselves a safe area and to remain calm. At that point, I had no idea whether the incident was real or not, but I knew I had to keep people safe. It wasn't easy, there were so many people running in all directions and it was impossible to get a visual on what was happening or where people were running from. But we managed to get control of the situation, kept everyone reassured and made the building safe until it was revealed it was a false alarm.

Looking back, it was actually quite a useful exercise, as it made us think about the security arrangements for the building and what steps we needed to take in case of a real terrorist attack. I had stepped up and dealt with it and had done so without triggering any of the flashbacks or darker moments I'd been through. That felt good. It showed me I'd moved on.

It showed me as well, that I might have been working on Civvy Street for a while now, but all those old army instincts would always still be there. You can take the man out of the military, it seems, but you can never quite take the military out of the man.

ACKNOWLEDGEMENTS

I would like to thank:

Sir Lloyd Dorfman CBE
Jake Irwin
Olly Olsen
Charlie Green
Nick Goble and Tom Bromley

Without your support I would not be able to tell my story.